A Victor's Tale

The Story of Milo Flaten: One of the GIs Who
Led the Invasion of Omaha Beach on D-Day

DOC WESTRING

Paperback ISBN: 979-8-9863671-0-1
Ebook ISBN: 979-8-9863671-1-8

Cover and interior design © by Bespoke Book Covers
Maps and charts © Alex McDonald
Author's photo: Grace Lennon Photography
All other photos furnished by Milo Flaten except on page 151, which was furnished by the author.

Independently published by Doc Westring in the United States.
First Edition 2022
www.docwestring.com

*This book is dedicated to all the men and
women of the Greatest Generation who
in any way, on the battlefield or the home
front, contributed to the Allies' victory
in World War II.*

*I hate war as only a soldier who has
lived it can, only as one who has seen
its brutality, its futility, its stupidity.*

General Dwight D. Eisenhower

Contents

T/Sgt. Milo G. Flaten, Jr. in Paris, France, 1945

Prologue

A 19-year-old army private named Milo G. Flaten, Jr. stood nervously in the bow of a small landing craft approaching shore. Bullets pinged as they hit the upraised steel ramp in front of him. His little boat led a huge armada of ships and landing craft crossing the English Channel, heading for a French beach code-named Omaha. His vessel jarred to a sudden stop, the ramp lowered, and Milo jumped into the water. He immediately sank to the bottom under the weight of the heavy gear he carried. Coming up for air several times amid bullets zipping into the water all around him, he shed everything but his shoes, pants, and shirt. Trained never to give up his rifle, he held it in one hand and began swimming the three hundred yards to the beach.

Approaching water's edge, he hid behind one of the metal tank-traps on the beach to avoid rifle and machine gun fire coming his way. There were no other Americans around; nobody in front, to either side, or behind him. They had told him tanks would be there clearing the way, but he saw none. He was soaking wet on a dismally cold rainy morning, crouching in a frigid sea in a state of utter terror. Soon, bodies washed up next to him and a while later, some live soldiers joined him.

In the coming months, his mind would be wholly occupied with fighting and surviving. It didn't dawn on him until much later that he might have been the first Allied soldier to land on Omaha Beach on D-Day. Fifty years would pass before he'd give much thought to that possibility.

Introduction

I met Milo Flaten (pronounced Flay-ten) in 2002 when I joined a band in Madison, Wisconsin, some 75 miles west of my Milwaukee home. We played traditional jazz one night a week in a hotel lobby bar and had a fairly regular audience, most of whom were members of the local jazz society. Milo was almost always there, often whistling along to the songs we played, to the annoyance of some and amusement of others. I was familiar with his name but had never met him before. We were both lawyers, and I had seen mention of him in State Bar publications. I remembered the name because I thought it so unusual; I'd never known anyone named Milo or heard the last name Flaten. Later, I found out Flaten was a very common Norwegian name meaning meadow or flatland. Milo was then 77 years old, totally bald, fit, and trim with no paunch. He stood over six feet tall—an unusual height for a man of his generation. Except for prominent hearing aids, I thought he seemed quite a bit younger than his age. On summer nights when he drove up to the hotel with his girlfriend in a jaunty, open sports car, he looked decidedly dapper.

A few years later, a friend told me something about Milo's military background. The story was incorrect, but startling enough for me to check further. The truth was even more interesting than what I'd been told. Milo had been one of the first soldiers to land on Omaha Beach on D-Day—possibly the first. He lived through it and continued to fight (with several potentially lethal interruptions) until the war in Europe was over. I was more than interested. I knew World War II veterans were dying off at a rapid rate and their stories were being lost to posterity. Milo's tale was one that needed to be shared and remembered.

In our initial talks I found his life to have an eerie "Forrest Gump" component to it.[1] There wasn't any aspect of the limited mental ability the Gump character presented, but at every turn, Milo was linked to well-known occurrences and famous people. Accomplishments throughout his life were at an impressive and unusual level. (Someone else had told Milo he was a brilliant Forrest Gump; he rented and watched the movie and was quite amused by it.)

Like many veterans, he didn't talk about the war after he returned to the States unless it was with other vets. He said normally he didn't even think about it. But when the fiftieth anniversary of D-Day came around in 1994, he was invited to give a speech about his experiences. When he started searching his memory, recollections came flooding in. He made the speech and continued to his tell stories thereafter, literally until the day he died. Most were about his experiences in World War II, but he talked about other subjects, too. He'd played college football and professional baseball and been a professional musician. He had continued his military career in the Army Reserve after WWII as a paratrooper and retired as a colonel. His sister married a movie actor and was in some films herself. He practiced trial law for years, then became a successful arbitrator. He had friends in high places, famous people he'd met and known. Almost every tale was as surprising and interesting as the prior one. His life story fascinated me, particularly his experiences in the war. It cried out to be written while he could still tell it.

Two others had started writing about him, but neither had carried through. He'd been interviewed several times by the press, radio, and television, and by several authors who used his comments in their books. He'd told some of his stories in speeches given in recent years, often wearing the uniform he wore when he retired from the Army. Yet no one had written his biography or even an account of what I considered the most striking part of his life— his military service during wartime. I offered to do it, and Milo agreed.

When I began interviewing him, Milo was 83 and having some difficulty remembering. His walk was an older man's gait; by then he was somewhat stooped, bent at the waist. His zest for life had not dimmed, however. He was still dating and complaining that most of the women he'd gone out with had kicked him out (he called himself a "kickee"). He still worked full time, driving around the countryside holding arbitration hearings. He was on the board of directors of several organizations and businesses, including a bank, and volunteered with several groups supporting community better-ment. Though he no longer played an instrument (he had played sousaphone, string bass and bugle), he was an avid jazz fan, at-tending almost every traditional jazz and swing performance he could find within 100 miles. His love of sports took him to many basketball, baseball, and football games, often with his teenaged grandson. Those he couldn't get to, he watched on television. His was a full and interesting life. Even though he sometimes said he was getting dotty, his energy, intelligence, and vitality were evident.

Like all of us, Milo was the product of his times and the parenting he received. His father and mother were born in the Victo-rian era and were, to a large extent, Victorian people. Milo was much like his dad in that he was not in touch with his emotions. Not that he didn't have any, but like many men—especially men his age —he wasn't aware of or seemingly affected by them. That may have saved his mental health during and after his wartime service. Many otherwise strong and resourceful men totally lost it in combat when they reached their breaking point. People called it shell-shock in the First World War and battle-fatigue or combat-exhaustion in World War II. In the middle of battle, a man would suddenly stop fighting, start to cry, and become helpless. Others fought on without stopping, but suffered from various symptoms of post-traumatic stress disorder (PTSD) in the years following their military service.

As far as I could tell, Milo never reached his breaking point, even after months of the cruelest, bloodiest battles one can imagine. People and animals were blown apart in front of him. Again and again he killed and maimed other human beings, usually with his rifle or grenades, but also with a knife or his hands. He was terrified from his first day in combat until his last. After continuously facing death and being so fearful, one would think he must have run out of adrenaline.

I can't say whether he suffered from PTSD after his service. He told me he still occasionally had dreams about the war, most of which involved his hearing enemy tanks approaching. While bad dreams can be a symptom of PTSD, Milo's didn't appear to have a disabling effect on him. Yet I have to believe his experiences in combat had an enormous impact on his life. I can't imagine how any man or woman could remain unaffected by the shock, stress, and horror war presents.

While revealing much about his feelings didn't come easily to him, one emotion did come through often: he talked about feeling a sense of loneliness, of being a stranger. This seemed pervasive in his younger years and during his WWII service. It likely abated after he married and had a family, but was noticeable again in the years after his wife's death. Other than his intense fear during combat, it is the one emotion he could recognize and describe. Otherwise, he was a pragmatic man, doing whatever was necessary to get a job done. If there were feelings involved, he didn't talk about them, or maybe never perceived them.

One other thing about him impressed me greatly. It was not an emotion, but it was a constant throughout his life: the man had unbelievable good luck. Granted, he had his share of terrible experiences and rough times, but he almost always came out of them favorably.

Milo was highly intelligent, at times acerbic, and clearly did not suffer fools gladly. When I met with him, he was often outspoken, frequently profane, more than confident of his opinions, and not at all afraid to voice them emphatically. He was always serious when we worked together, and I never felt he was a funny man. It startled me to hear from his friends that in his younger days he'd had a robust sense of humor, with one even describing it as wicked. His bearing when I was present was, not surprisingly, that of a military officer. At his funeral his daughter described him in her eulogy as having a twinkle in his eye, a song in his heart, and a smile on his face. That was a Milo I never met, a man I couldn't write about, although I certainly would have liked to. I've seen photos of that man, clowning around with his buddies, laughing with his family, raising a glass in good cheer, and I wish I had known him. It seems Milo transformed during the latter years of his life. His sense of humor and enjoyment of silliness left him, and he viewed the world almost two-dimensionally. He had always held strong opinions and was never shy about voicing them, but now he appeared to have lost his graciousness and tolerance of others' beliefs. He monopolized conversations with his own viewpoints and argued vigorously with anyone who disagreed. People became uncomfortable around him and stopped seeking his company. Friends faded away, and gradually he lost most of his old pals and drinking buddies. One colleague who didn't drift away said Milo's attitude and behavior didn't bother him and he stayed close, but he was well aware others felt uneasy in Milo's presence.

I thought Milo treated me as an equal, although he was all business, with no humor or light-heartedness shown. It surprised me to discover we had been members of the same college fraternity and lived in the same chapter house, though ten or more years apart. That didn't interest him at all. His lack of warmth made it obvious I was there to do a job and not to establish a friendship.

I need to note one other aspect of Milo's personality. His children told me they heard his stories repeated often over the years and realized they substantially improved with time. That caused me to wonder if facts he related to me might be inflated or erroneous, or his memories might have included someone else's experience as his own. For instance, my brother (who was in an organization with Milo) had been with him when someone mentioned Bastogne and the Battle of the Bulge. My brother told me Milo commented some-thing to the effect that "I was never so cold as I was in Bastogne." In truth, Milo never was at Bastogne or in the Battle of the Bulge. When those events occurred, he was in England, and later in Paris. So, you might ask, could there be other instances of lily-gilding in this account? That certainly is possible. Several times I found something he told me to be questionable or even obviously incorrect. I couldn't tell whether it came from a faulty 83-year-old memory or a desire to spin a more memorable yarn, but I've done what fact-checking I could. Sometimes I've commented in a note on what I found problematical. In some cases, I have corrected his recollections. In other instances, I've left his memories as he recalled them, and noted the matter in a note. I mention this not to cast judgment on Milo, but in case a reader finds a contradiction or discrepancy. Being of a certain age myself, I can appreciate how difficult it is to recall events from my life sixty or more years ago. What I present here is what Milo told me he remembered, with assistance from his family and friends, and some historical refer-ences.[2]

Chapter 1

Bizarre Days

Milo Flaten's first day in the Army was not going well. He was having trouble with his initial assignment, taking the General Classification Test. Somewhat like an IQ Test, the Army used it to assign an inductee to a specialty, such as artillery, aviation, or infantry. Milo was a smart young man who earned excellent grades throughout his school experience. In fact, he was so bright he scored high enough on an Army Specialized Training Program Test (ASTP) that he was to be sent to college during his years of military service. There were concerns that at the war's end there wouldn't be enough educated men to lead the nation, and some smart young men were chosen to be college-trained. Milo's problem with *this* test was not a lack of intelligence. It was his ability to get questions answered before he had to run outside and throw up. He was hopelessly drunk.

The day had begun well. That morning, June 6, 1943, Milo graduated from Shorewood High, a suburban school in metropolitan Milwaukee. He had turned 18 a month earlier and received notice his induction into the Army would take place the same day as commencement. He must have had mixed emotions as they handed him his diploma, feeling proud of his scholastic accomplishments, yet contemplating what was to come. His dad, Mike, couldn't get off work to attend, but Winnie, his mom, was there. He met her outside the school after the ceremony, handed her his cap and gown, and reminded her to get them back to the rental agency in time to avoid a late penalty. She gave him enough money for the streetcar fare—fifteen cents. They exchanged a hug and kiss, and Milo left for the induction center, a warehouse in downtown Milwaukee. It would be a long and worrisome time before Winnie and Mike would have their boy home again.

The problem with Milo's intoxication had started innocently enough at the induction center where the draftees were getting a physical exam. They were naked or in their underwear, visiting station after station where examiners looked at one part of their body or another. Medics and soldiers in charge were all clothed, but Milo saw several other men in suits and snap-brim hats standing against a wall. He wondered who they were and what they were doing there. One man's suit coat fell open and Milo thought he saw a pistol. The mystery was soon solved. The fully dressed observers were guards from the Wisconsin State Reformatory in Green Bay, then the state's prison for juveniles. They were guarding some prisoners going through the induction process. As the war ground on, the Army badly needed more replacements. Selected inmates were being granted parole if they volunteered and were accepted into the armed forces.

Milo was in excellent shape: he was athletic, six feet tall, and weighed 155 pounds. The doctors could find nothing wrong with him and declared him fit for duty. Later that afternoon Milo G. Flaten, Jr. raised his right hand, swore an oath, and became a private in the Army of the United States.[1] He boarded a bus with other inductees and was driven to the Milwaukee Road Railway Depot. There, he got on a train headed for his first Army base, Camp Grant, about 100 miles to the southwest in Rockford, Illinois.

After riding awhile, Milo got bored and took a stroll around the train. He discovered the club car, preferred it to the coach where he'd been sitting, and took a seat. The prison parolees were also sitting there. Later the train stopped at a small town, and the inductees had to change trains. The Reformatory boys took advantage of the stop to find a nearby liquor store and buy a bottle of whiskey. Once on board their new train, the boys opened the bottle, passed it around, and offered Milo a drink. He'd had a few beers in his young life, but was not, in any sense, an experienced drinker. He thanked them but declined their offer. That sparked a round of teasing, gibes like "What, do you think you're better than us?" "What's the matter, don't you want to hang around with jailbirds?" After a few more taunts, Milo gave in and joined them, and they included him thereafter each time the bottle went around. He was soon quite drunk and needed help to get to the base. Results from the exam he took when he arrived were pitiful; his score indicated he was an ignoramus.

The Army brass in charge were bewildered. They didn't understand how anyone so stupid could have qualified to go to college, and had no idea what to do with Milo. Normally, a recruit would be shipped out in a matter of days, but they kept Milo there for several weeks, not knowing where to send him. They gave him uniforms and required him to learn how to act like a soldier—who to salute, what insignia indicated what rank, etc.—but he was given no assigned duty. He hung around the base, went into town to see movies, and rode the train to Milwaukee and back on weekends. He was bored and frustrated. Finally, somebody made a decision, and Milo was told they had assigned him to Fort Hamilton, in Brooklyn, New York. He thought he might be going to Brooklyn College, but that was not to be. The only criteria the Army had to evaluate him was his low test score, and they assumed he was of borderline intelligence.

Fort Hamilton was home to the 113th Infantry Regiment, made up of New York and New Jersey National Guard units. Its members were almost all Italian-Americans. Milo was taller than nearly everyone there and one of the few whose last name didn't end in a vowel. Many of the troops regularly spoke Italian, and he didn't understand a word of what they were saying. He felt awkward and isolated. Before long, though, he became friends with two of the men, Danny Rinaldi and Marco DeSantis. They took Milo under their wing, translated for him when necessary, and made him feel a part of the group. One weekend, they took Milo with them when they visited Marco's home in Newark. Before they got there, DeSantis told Milo his mama didn't trust non-Italians, so he couldn't be "My-low Flay-ten." He would have to be "Mee-lo Fla-tee-na," (spoken with an Italian accent). Marco introduced Milo to his mother, a tiny lady, perhaps all of four feet six inches. Milo towered over her. "Meelo Flateena," she said, "that's a primo Italian name." Danny and Marco thought it hilarious.

Milo's unit was assigned to walk beach patrols on Long Island, watching for enemy ships or invaders. The sergeant issued them guard dogs and Browning Automatic Rifles (BARs) but gave them no training. A BAR was an automatic weapon, a large rifle which fired automatically, like a machine gun, but they gave him just a few bullets. Milo had fired a shotgun and a .22 rifle before, but only a few times. He wasn't sure what the Army expected of him if he discovered a submarine or invaders running up the beach. He guessed he'd run for a payphone and call the camp if anything happened.

It soon became clear to Milo some of the soldiers he was serving with were of a less than honest bent. There were some signs his friends Danny and Marco had been involved in illegal exploits before they joined up, but the low level of honesty of others in the outfit was more obvious. For instance, some enjoyed breaking into vacant cottages and homes along the shore and stealing whatever they could find. Milo was not happy about that. Nor was he pleased with his assigned dog, Rex, a Doberman Pinscher. Rex was supposed to heel while on patrol, but the animal preferred to run out in the ocean and play. Milo tried to keep him under control, but Rex refused to obey. He resisted commands and took to biting Milo's legs above the top of his leggins.[2] Soon his trousers were shredded. When he came back from patrol, the sergeant yelled, "Flaten, what the hell are you doing out there? Your pants are always torn." Milo did his best to explain the dog was to blame.

About three weeks after Milo arrived, the rest of the men in his unit became convinced their duty was simply too demanding and decided their best course of action would be to go on strike. It astounded Milo how incredibly stupid they were. Even as a raw recruit, he knew the Army wouldn't tolerate a strike. In fact, failing to do one's job would amount to dereliction of duty, a serious, punishable offense. The other men didn't seem to comprehend that, and one day simply stopped going to the kennels to get their dogs. Predictably, the Army was more than irritated. It held court-martial proceedings and was about to send everyone, Milo included, to a military prison on Long Island.

Milo was understandably upset and knew he had to do something quickly. At Camp Grant, he'd attended church services occasionally, more out of boredom than religious fervor. The chaplain had said they should contact him if they had any problems. Not knowing what else to do, Milo sought out the chaplain at Fort Hamilton. He told the padre about the college program and what happened when he took the Army's placement test. "And I don't know what this strike is all about," he said. "Half the time those guys aren't even speaking English." The chaplain interceded and arranged for another General Classification test. Milo passed with a high score and was reassigned. He would go to college after all, to John B. Stetson University in DeLand, Florida.

DeLand was a pleasant small city about 26 miles inland from Daytona Beach. When Milo arrived it was summer, not the most attractive season to visit Florida, but he didn't mind. He was eager to do something positive after all the delays and odd experiences he'd encountered. He arrived at Stetson and put his barracks bag down on the floor by the first sergeant's desk. The man looked up and asked, "What are you doing here?"

"I'm ready to go to college," Milo replied, showing his orders and ASTP card.

"They've closed down the program," the sergeant said. "They don't have it anymore." Milo asked why he'd been sent there then. The sergeant told him some parts of the Army were slow in picking up on the information. He said newspapers had published articles about it for weeks. The Allies were fighting in Italy and experiencing heavy losses, and the Army had changed its policy. As much as the nation would need educated leaders in years to come, sending replacement troops to Italy had become more important. But the sergeant said even though the program was being terminated, Milo could stay there. All personnel presently in the program were allowed to finish their current semester before being assigned elsewhere. That was not particularly helpful to Milo since he'd arrived long after the semester had started, but he attended his classes anyway. He wore his uniform and marched with other ASTP students to each assigned room. He had no books, nor any idea what his instructors were talking about. The civilian students, as well as those in the ASTP program, were all weeks or months ahead of him in each course.

But Milo discovered the classrooms had two doors, one opening onto the central hallway, and the other to the outside. He spent the rest of his brief career at Stetson walking in from the hall and out the exterior door. There he would sit in the sunshine and watch coeds play tennis on a nearby court. When the period ended, he'd march to his next class, walk outside, and watch more tennis. Before long, though, he lost interest—even in the girls. Once again, he was bored and frustrated. This wasn't what he thought being in either the military or college would be like. Finally, the semester ended, and someone in command decided Private Flaten ought to go through Basic Training. That seemed appropriate to Milo; he'd been in the Army for over three months without it.

Chapter 2

Brass Tacks

An army is successful in battle only if its soldiers persevere. They must continue to fight despite overwhelming odds and potentially superior forces. Most of us have no desire to experience battle. Putting oneself in danger of injury or death goes against the basic human instinct for self-preservation. The body's built-in reaction to danger is fight or flight. Flight doesn't work well for armies. It results in people hiding from combat, retreating against orders, or worse, deserting. The U.S. Army's Basic Training program (casually called boot camp) was designed to counter one's natural inclinations. Its goal was to instill in soldiers the belief they simply couldn't run away from peril. They had to keep fighting no matter how great the dangers or meager their chances, and then they would always prevail. That required a complete transformation of thought for virtually every recruit. Each had to learn to respond automatically to orders and act in concert with his cohorts, without question or hesitation. A change of that magnitude required constant, strenuous, repetitious drilling. That, plus learning a host of new skills and tactics, was what Milo was about to experience.

Many young men entering the Army were nervous, wondering

what Basic Training might be like. For several reasons, Milo wasn't. He was a tough, resilient kid, having grown up in hard conditions during the Great Depression. Although his father, Mike, was a lawyer, the family didn't have much money. His dad had opened his own law office in Minneapolis in 1920, and although he still had clients after the stock market crashed, many were unable to pay their legal bills. A year or so after the Depression started, Mike had to close his office. He got a job as a lawyer with the U.S. Department of Agriculture, which kept the family afloat but required them to move several times as a result of transfers.

Milo, his parents, and sister Cathy[1], five years older than he, lived in a cold, drafty house in Minneapolis. Milo slept up in the unheated attic. Minnesota winters being wickedly frigid, the Flatens had to learn to make do and cope without. Finances got so tight one winter the city turned off their water for failure to pay their utility bill. Winnie sent little Milo outside to collect clean snow, which she would melt on the stove for drinking water. He learned early in his life how to deal with adversities.

In high school, knowing military service awaited them at eighteen, Milo and his friend "Andy" Anders[2] joined a volunteer civilian-military program. It met at an armory, where the boys learned basic military skills like how to march and drill with a rifle—close-order drill, the Army called it. The boys both also learned to play an old bugle Andy's dad owned. They used it to practice the various bugle calls Milo had heard at Boy Scout camps he'd attended: first call, reveille, taps, mess call, and the rest.

Milo was an aggressive, strapping athlete, having taken part in football, baseball, competitive swimming, and tennis. He was in great shape and, at six feet, was taller than most adult men. He had also matured as a member of the adult workforce while in his teens. With the great number of males leaving for military service, local bands and orchestras found themselves without players able to perform their music. Milo was an exceptional string bass player for his age and soon was out most weekends earning good money as a musician. What's more, he'd already been in the Army for almost three months and was an experienced soldier. He felt he had little to worry about in Basic Training.

In mid-September, he left DeLand and traveled about a hundred miles north to Camp Blanding at Starke, Florida, to begin his seventeen weeks of Basic. They assigned him to C Company, one of four companies in the 190th Training Battalion. Most of the other recruits in his unit came from southern Illinois, from rural homes, the sons of farmers and coal miners. They had distinctive southern accents, the thickest Milo had ever encountered. He had great difficulty understanding them and considered them "dumb." With that attitude, he made few friends and felt isolated and sorely out of place.

As the recruits learned how to fall into formation and march, the instructors also began orienting them to the Army and the way it operated. While Milo had received a lot of that information in the past few months, most recruits had little knowledge of how the Army operated. They learned its Table of Organization and military courtesy: the Army ranks and who to salute and call "sir." They, themselves, were privates (Pvt.); in army slang, they were called buck privates, indicating the lowest rank in the Army. After a man completed Basic Training, he might sometime thereafter be promoted to Private First Class (Pfc.)— although that was not guaranteed. To denote his new rank, he would receive one chevron, informally called a stripe, to wear on his upper sleeve. The promotion promised a little higher pay and status, but granted the man no more authority than he had as a private, which was essentially none. He was not authorized to command any other soldiers.

However, the rank above Pfc., corporal (Cpl.), did confer upon the soldier some authority. Corporals and sergeants were called noncommissioned officers, or NCOs. They were authorized to hold positions that allowed them to give commands to other men—men who were below them in rank. For instance, if a unit led by a sergeant had its leader wounded or killed, a corporal could be appointed to take the leader position without being promoted. A private or Pfc. could not, as he was not permitted to command anyone.

Corporals wore two stripes on their sleeves; The next highest in rank, sergeants, (in slang, buck sergeants), the lowest of the several sergeant ranks, wore three. The insignia of the next highest in rank, the staff sergeant (S/Sgt.) was the buck sergeant's three stripes plus a rocker, an arc below the stripes which connected to them. Next higher was a technical sergeant (T/Sgt.), (usually called a tech sergeant) who wore three stripes and two rockers. Above him in rank was a first sergeant (1st Sgt.), who added a lozenge, or diamond, between the tech sergeant's stripes and rockers. And finally, there was the master sergeant (M/Sgt.), who wore three stripes and three rockers. (Someone familiar with a more modern army might be confused about who technical sergeants were; the rank was abolished after WWII and replaced with sergeant first class, or SFC.)

Again, corporals and sergeants were non-commissioned officers. There was another group above them in rank called Warrant Officers, who were generally specialists in some specific field. They were also NCOs; but as Milo had little contact with them, will not be described in detail here.

Commissioned officers were those who had a bachelor's degree, completed specialized officer training, and received a commission, an appointment to an officer's position. Some were trained at service academies, such as West Point. Others were in the Army ROTC (Reserve Officer Training Corps) programs held at many colleges. Many attended Officer Candidate Schools run by the Army. And, during WWII when officer ranks dwindled due to death or injury, some capable, experienced sergeants were sent back behind the lines to specialized, accelerated schools that lasted several weeks, and returned to combat as second lieutenants, the lowest ranking commissioned officer. However, when the war ended those appointees reverted to enlisted status if they stayed in the Army or Reserve.

U.S. ARMY PERSONNEL IN WWII
(In Increasing Order of Rank, Excepting Warrant Officers)

ENLISTED	**Abbrev.**	**Insignia (upper sleeve)**
Private	Pvt	None
Private 1st Class	Pfc	1 chevron (stripe)
Corporal	Cpl	2 chevrons
Sergeant	Sgt	3 chevrons,
Staff Sergeant	S/Sgt	3 chevrons, 1 rocker
Tech Sergeant	T/Sgt	3 chevrons, 2 rockers
First Sergeant	1st Sgt	3 chevrons, 3 rockers separated by a lozenge
Master Sergeant	M/Sgt	3 chevrons, 3 rockers

COMMISSIONED OFFICERS

Company Grade	**Abbrev.**	**Insignia**
Second Lieutenant	2nd Lt.	1 gold bar*
First Lieutenant	1st Lt.	1 silver bar*
Captain	Cpt	2 silver bars*

Field Grade		
Major	Maj.	Gold oak leaf**
Lieutenant Colonel	Lt. Col.	Silver oak leaf**
Colonel	Col.	Silver eagle**

General Officers		
Brigadier General	Brig. Gen.	1 star**
Major General	Maj. Gen.	2 stars**
Lieutenant General	Lt. Gen.	3 stars**
General	Gen.	4 stars**
General of the Army	GA	5 stars**

*worn on shoulder

** worn on collar

Second lieutenants (2nd Lt.) wore a gold bar on their shoulder as an indication of their rank. They could give orders to any enlisted (non-commissioned) soldier. Their immediate superior was a first lieutenant (1st Lt.), who wore a silver bar. Next in command was a captain (Cpt.), who wore two silver bars on his shoulder. These three ranks were called Company Grade officers, and in the infantry were usually on the front line, commanding GIs in combat. Consequently, many were killed and injured; replacements were almost always needed.

The three next highest in rank were called Field Grade officers. Though they might at times be in or near combat, they were more often back at the unit's headquarters location planning, strategizing, and commanding. The lowest ranked of this group was a major (Maj.), who wore a gold oak leaf on his collar (all Field Grade and General Officers wore their insignia on their collar). Superior to the major was a lieutenant colonel (Lt. Col.), (colonel is pronounced "kernel"). who wore a silver oak leaf. Highest ranked of the group was a colonel (Col.) whose insignia was a silver eagle.

Finally, there were the general officers, whose rank was indicated by stars on their collars. One star indicated a brigadier general (Brig. Gen.). Major generals (Maj. Gen.) wore two stars. Three stars indicated a lieutenant general (Lt. Gen.), while four identified a general, (Gen.) usually the highest ranked general officer. There were several exceptions to this: five men were elevated to five-star general, including Dwight Eisenhower in 1944, and Omar Bradley, the last to be so appointed, in 1950. General officers were the leaders of the Army at its highest levels, and were responsible for overall command of all the soldiers in their respective units. In addition to absorbing the above, recruits (often called "boots," from "boot camp,"), also had to learn the organization of the Army, and how their position fit into it. As Milo was to become an infantryman, this discussion will be limited to infantry units. Airborne, armored, and other branches had their own particular configurations.

The largest infantry organization with a permanent personnel configuration was called a division. It was made up of a number of subsidiary groups in line with the Army's reliance on the factor of three. The next smallest infantry group was an infantry regiment, and each division contained three of them. Divisions had other components as well. For instance, the one Milo would join, the 29th Infantry Division, also included a mechanized reconnaissance troop, a combat engineer battalion, a medical battalion, four artillery battalions, a light maintenance company, quartermaster company, signal company, military police platoon, band, and headquarters company. Regardless, the identifying feature of most Army infantry formations was that they included three of the next smallest units as part of their makeup. Consequently, each infantry regiment contained three infantry battalions. Each battalion contained three companies. Every company contained three platoons, and every platoon included three squads. The squad was the smallest permanent unit in the Army. This format was chosen, in part, from the realization that the most mobility and speed could be gained by having two units fighting and one in reserve.

As a result of its experiences in WWI, the Army decided the most soldiers one man could control and command effectively was ten. As a result, they made the squad the basic unit of the infantry. A squad was a group of ten soldiers led by a squad leader (a staff sergeant) and his assistant (a sergeant). Squad members had different primary assignments: three made up a BAR team, two were designated as scouts, and five were riflemen. However, each squad member had to know the job of every other squad member. He also had to learn to be a squad leader and assistant squad leader, as someone would have to take over if those leaders were killed or wounded.

U.S. ARMY INFANTRY ORGANIZATION WWII

UNIT	COMPOSITION	AUTH. STRENGTH	COMMANDER
Rifle Squad	Twelve Riflemen	12	S/Sgt.
Rifle Platoon	Three Rifle Squads	41	2nd Lt.
Rifle Company	Three Rifle Platoons	193	Cpt.
Infantry Battalion	Three Rifle Companies	860	Lt. Col.
Infantry Regiment	Three Infantry Battalions	3,118	Col.
Infantry Division	Three Infantry Regiments	14,253	Maj. Gen.
Corps	Two + Infantry Divisions	Varied	Maj. Gen.
Army	Two + Corps	Varied	Lt. Gen. or Gen.
Army Group	Two + Armies	Varied	Gen.

Three rifle squads plus a few other components made up a rifle platoon, a formation authorized to have up to 41 members. It was led by the platoon leader, a first or second lieutenant, whose assistant was the platoon sergeant, usually a tech sergeant. Three rifle platoons (plus other units) made up a rifle company, up to 193 soldiers led by a captain. Three rifle companies (plus others) constituted an infantry battalion authorized to consist of 860 soldiers. It was commanded by a lieutenant colonel. Three of those battalions (plus other units) made up a regiment, a body of up to 3,118 men under the command of a colonel. And three infantry regiments (plus others, as noted) made up an infantry division, authorized to have as many as 14,253 men. Divisions were commanded by major (two-star) generals.

There were additional units larger than divisions, but their makeup could change with each new assignment. Next largest was a Corps (pronounced "core") which was comprised of two or more divisions. A corps was led by a major (two-star) general, and designated by Roman numerals, such as IV Corps, or XIII Corps. Two or more corps made up an Army (such as the Third Army or Sixth Army, etc.) Armies were commanded by lieutenant (three-star) generals or (four-star) generals. And, finally, there were Army Groups, which consisted of two or more Armies, and were commanded by a general or lieutenant general. There was only one Army Group in the European Theater of Operations (ETO); it contained all Armies located there, and was commanded by Gen. Omar Bradley.

The training cadre intentionally did not make life in boot camp easy for the trainees. Their charges, boys and young men, were being prepared for a mentality and lifestyle of toughness and grit in which they would live like animals and kill human beings. There were no luxuries. Their basic needs were anticipated and supplied by the Army. For example, their meals and clothes were furnished to them (commissioned officers had to purchase theirs). Their daily training uniforms were dungarees made of green herringbone tweed with a billed cap somewhat like a baseball cap. They were issued leather boots they were supposed to shine, but they found that impossible. No matter how hard they tried, the rough leather wouldn't take a gloss. They also received ODs, olive drab uniforms to be worn when on leave and for certain formal drill formations. ODs included dress trousers, shirt, tie, shoes, and a cloth garrison (or overseas) cap, which looked somewhat like an inverted, open business envelope.

They lived in rough, single-story wooden barracks called "hutments." The buildings had screened windows but no glass panes, and no device to close them. There was a coal or wood stove at each end of the building. When temperatures dropped, the men put boards over the windows to keep heat in, but that didn't help much. Milo's seventeen weeks didn't end until January, 1944, and January overnight temperatures in Jacksonville are often below freezing. Milo would remember it as one of the colder winters he ever experienced.

Training was from 7:30 to 5:00 every day, and it began immediately after the newcomers arrived in camp. As they left their bus, they were ordered to line up—and not just haphazardly. They were to line up by height, from tallest to shortest. From the first day of Basic to the last, they always lined up for formations, and always by height. Milo, at six feet, was always the tallest, and, consequently, first in line. The trainers appointed him Guidon Bearer (or Guide), the man who carried the company's Guidon, or flag. He stood in front of the company alongside the commander and was the rallying point for troops to fall into formation. Being out front, he responded to the marching orders given, while the other men guided on him and the banner he carried.

Various bugle calls punctuated and regulated the days in boot camp. A bugler played his horn into a microphone, which broadcast the sound all over camp. The earliest call of each day, first call, rousted the men out of bed. The next, reveille, was played as the camp's flag was raised. Throughout the day there were mess calls, sick calls, duty calls, etc. Call for retreat was at six. Everyone stood at attention and saluted, even though the actual flag ceremony might be happening half a mile away and out of their sight. The bugler played call to colors, and an honor squad lowered the flag. Next, they fired a cannon. There was another mess call, a call to quarters, and finally, taps at lights out. Milo's ability with a bugle became known, and he was named assistant bugler, which had its good points and bad. When he had bugle duty he was excused from some drilling, which he appreciated. However, he also had to be the first one up in the morning and the last one to bed at night, and was usually tired as a result.

The Army knew soldiers in combat needed to be in top physical condition. Recruits constantly did pushups and other calisthenics (called PT, or physical training) to get in shape. They also did pushups as a punishment for rule infractions—or for just irritating a superior. Marching was also emphasized in the early days of camp. Cadets learned and practiced close-order drill, marching in ranks with their units as well as in larger formations with other groups. In addition to building strength, it taught the newcomers to act automatically and in sync. They had to master keeping in step and rhythm while displaying or carrying their rifles in various positions. Every Friday afternoon there was a formal retreat where the entire battalion would parade wearing their ODs. Then there were field marches, cross-country hikes that went on for miles—usually with weapons and full packs. Sometimes they'd march along a road. Other times they'd go cross-country, often through rough terrain. In the cross-country marches, they used "open step," meaning they didn't march to a cadence as they did on the parade grounds. Milo took part in one night-march with full heavy packs that went for eighteen miles; another during daytime lasted twenty-two miles. There were also exercises called motor marches or shuttle marches. Trucks would carry the troops about five miles. They'd get out and march cross-country for five miles. More trucks would pick them up, drive another five miles, and again they'd disembark and march another five. The process was repeated until they arrived back at camp. Some days they marched until they thought they would drop. It seemed like punishment at the time, but they would discover that combat demanded much more strength and stamina than Basic Training.

Eventually, a ragtag bunch of youngsters would come together as a military unit, acting more like soldiers than teenagers. They marched in cadence and order, took commands without question, and responded at once, without thinking. At that point, their training in military skills started: subjects like map and compass reading, night navigation by the stars, combat tactics, and weaponry. All these were important, but weaponry led the list.

Each man had to become completely familiar with the .30 caliber M1 Garand rifle, the infantryman's primary weapon. In this case, familiarity meant a high level of intimacy. Recruits were trained to consider their rifle as their best friend—the only friend they could completely rely on. They disassembled and reassembled their rifles three and four times a day until they could do it blindfolded. They needed to be able to do this in the dark of night, in the actual world of battle. If their weapon didn't work, they had to clean and repair it under any condition, night or day, rain or shine. Without it, they'd be close to helpless against an enemy.

They received two weeks of dry-run training on the rifle range (without ammunition), learning how to sight their weapon, how to squeeze the trigger, and how to shoot from standing, sitting, and prone (on their stomach) positions. They practiced finding the sight picture (aiming properly) and dry firing. At the same time, they began training on the hand grenade range. The most common grenades used in WWII were Mk IIs, fragmentation (or frag) grenades: small, oval bombs close to the size of a baseball (nicknamed pineapples for their appearance). They consisted of a heavy, dimpled cast-iron casing containing explosives, shrapnel, and a fuse mechanism. An attached handle was kept in place by a pin, preventing the device from exploding by accident. Pulling the pin freed the handle. Throwing the grenade allowed the handle to spring open and drop off, setting off a primer which in turn ignited an internal fuse. When the fuse burned down to the detonator, the grenade would explode, spewing jagged shards of hot metal as much as fifty yards in all directions. The entire process, from throwing to explosion, took somewhere around five seconds. For some reason, recruits were taught in boot camp to throw grenades as if they were a shot put, but once in combat the men would find that ineffective. They ignored their instructions and used several types of throws: underarm, side-arm, overhand, or a typical baseball throw. Milo wanted to save his arm for pitching, so he developed and used his own unique style. And Mk IIs were not always thrown. With an adaptor attached to his M1 rifle, a soldier could fire the device as a rifle grenade, giving it added height and range.

Another type of grenade was the WP (or Willy Peter, which stood for white phosphorous.) The element phosphorus will burn without an ignition source when exposed to air. When a WP grenade exploded it spit burning fragments of phosphorus outward, causing anyone struck by the chemical to suffer serious burns and possibly catch on fire. WP grenades, mortars, and artillery shells were also used to create smoke screens, as the burning element gives off an extensive amount of white smoke. A third type of grenade was an incendiary device called a thermal grenade. When set off, a chemical reaction produced heat, causing thermite powder in the device to ignite. The resulting heat was high enough to cut through metal or weld metal parts together—the burn could reach temperatures as high as $4,000 \, ^\circ F$.

Although it isn't a grenade, one other weapon, the Bangalore torpedo, needs to be described here, as it will be of interest later. It was designed to clear a path through barbed wire defenses and also to detonate landmines. It consisted of a metal pipe about two inches in diameter and five feet long, threaded at both ends, and filled with explosives. More pipes of the same size, but without explosives, could be screwed to the one carrying the charge. The elongation made it easier to set the pipe in place while under fire, and also carried the explosion farther from the GI handling it. For some reason Milo was not trained on this weapon.

After finishing dry firing practice, the trainees began shooting their M1s with live ammunition. They practiced hitting targets at distances of 150, 300, and 500 yards, using all three positions: standing, sitting, and lying prone. The primary position, prone, used the rifle's leather sling to hold it still and on target. Milo had excellent eyesight and muscle coordination and quickly achieved "expert" status with his rifle. During this training, the men also practiced affixing and using their bayonet—a long knife which could be attached to the end of the rifle's barrel. The modified weapon could be used much like a spear.

Trainees also practiced firing carbines, the rifles that officers carried. Lighter than M1s and with shorter barrels, they also shot .30 caliber ammunition, but their bullets were smaller and the guns less accurate. Carbines also were also not nearly as valuable in close-in fighting. The M1, with its heavier weight and strong stock, was useful as a weapon in itself. Recruits were taught how to swing it and use it as a club.

Next, the men practiced with the .45 caliber semi-automatic pistol, the Thompson submachine gun (the infamous Tommy Gun used by gangsters in the 1920s), the BAR, and the M3 submachine gun. All but the .45 were shoulder-fired automatic weapons. Then they learned how to fire machine guns, both the air-cooled .30 caliber and the heavy .50 caliber weapon with a water jacket to cool it. Both of those weapons were mounted on a tripod stand. The rapid continuous fire of a machine gun causes its barrel to get extremely hot. The .30 caliber weapon had to be fired in short bursts in order prevent it from overheating and being damaged. Water in the jacket enclosing the barrel on the heavier gun effectively dissipated heat, allowing for longer bursts.

Then came intensive training with bazookas, hand-held recoilless anti-armor rocket launchers. The bazooka was a metal tube several feet long and two or three inches in diameter (they were modified during the war). It was placed on the shoulder of a kneeling or standing soldier who aimed it, much as he would aim a rifle. It fired rocket shells used to pierce tanks and other armored vehicles, or the walls of buildings. Bazookas were also effective at taking out machine gun emplacements too far away to reach with grenades.

Boots also practiced firing mortars, another type of rocket launcher. These, too, were hollow tubes, with one end attached to a plate that rested on the ground, and the other end pointing up in the air at an angle. A mortar shell dropped into the tube fired when it hit the firing pin in the tube's bottom, causing it to travel upwards in an arc. It exploded when it came to earth or hit something on the way.

Mortars had a range of about 2100 yards, and could be aimed higher in the air, making them effective against targets hidden behind trees or tall structures.

The troops received extensive training in close combat, hand-to-hand fighting, including unarmed tactics such as jiu-jitsu, and fighting with knives, sticks, batons—even improvised weapons like shovels. Milo thought it was completely unnecessary, and couldn't imagine he would ever need to use it. The men were also taught a series of signals that allowed them to communicate in daylight without speaking, and another system that provided voiceless communication at night.

Trainees had to attend personal hygiene classes, lectures, and movies about the possible consequences of sexual activity. The films graphically showed men suffering from horrible cases of venereal disease, and the lectures were about how to avoid those infections. The Army knew its young men were at the peak of their sexual potency and libido and wanted to keep every man healthy and available for combat. Condoms were regularly furnished to the troops along with their rations.

Along with all the above, the men trained in offensive maneuvers designed for an attacking army. The primary goal of the coming invasion was to kill as many Germans as possible and drive the rest out of France and the other occupied countries. The Allies would then make war on Germany until its annihilation or complete surrender. Thus, Allied troops would be expected to continue pushing forward, always on the offensive. The technique primarily promoted by the infantry to do this was called fire and maneuver. A unit (say a platoon), would divide into two groups. The first, call it group A, shot their rifles with enough firepower to make the enemy keep their heads down. This was known as suppressive fire (in the movies it's often called covering fire). Once they established suppressive fire, group B moved forward to a point farther ahead than group A. Group B then dug in and laid down suppressive fire, allowing group A to advance ahead of it. The men repeated these leapfrogging steps until they could go no farther in separate groups. The entire unit then formed one line, called a skirmish line, and continued to attack until the enemy was driven off, captured, or destroyed.

Certain soldiers had specialized roles in this process. Two members of the unit were picked by the CO to be scouts, designated as 1st scout and 2nd scout. Because the jobs were dangerous and tough, they were often rotated among several or all the unit's members. In other outfits the same men kept the jobs for extended periods. The scouts' task was to locate the enemy so fire and maneuver could begin. With the other men under cover, the 1st scout would run out to a point roughly a hundred to a hundred and fifty feet in front of his unit, rifle at the ready, searching for signs of the enemy. The infantry manual specified that the scout's mission was to "proceed boldly and aggressively." In Milo's mind, that meant the scout was expected to make himself a target and invite the Germans to shoot at him. While the Army might not have been that blunt about it, he believed that's what it boiled down to.

Assuming he discovered no enemy, the 1st scout took cover and signaled the 2nd scout forward. The 2nd scout ran up to the 1st, and the two waited there until the rest of the unit came forward to their position. They repeated these movements until they located enemy troops. Then, once both scouts and the entire unit came together again, they advanced using fire and maneuver. That was the process the textbooks described, and because the land around Camp Blanding was flat and without fences, these tactics worked well. The trainees also learned other maneuvers, such as the attack of a river crossing, the attack of fortified positions (such as a pillbox), and the attack at night. They practiced two types of combat patrols, one of which looked for the enemy in order to engage him. The other was called recon (reconnaissance) and was designed to get information and leave an area without being detected.

Recruits were next introduced to the foxhole. Men in battle need cover from enemy rifle and machine-gun fire, and also from artillery shells exploding near them. A hole in the ground provides suitable cover for all but direct artillery hits. With logs covering the hole, the men could even be somewhat protected from those. They practiced digging foxholes big enough for two men to lie down in and deep enough for cover. Unless there was a firefight going on, one man would sleep while the other stood guard. The ground around Camp Blanding was sandy soil and easy to excavate, allowing the men to dig holes without great effort. Foxholes were dug with one's entrenching tool, essentially a shovel with a short handle. The blade part folded back onto the handle when not in use, and the soldier carried the tool on his belt. As much as his rifle was his best friend, the entrenching tool must have been a close second. It provided him with cover, and could also be used as a pickaxe and a weapon.

During the first five weeks of Basic, drilling was constant, and recruits were not granted furloughs (usually called "leaves"). They were required to stay in camp. Thereafter they were eligible for leaves on weekends and could go into town. The city of Jacksonville was about 50 miles northeast, and St. Augustine was about 55 miles due east; they were obvious destinations. While having weekends off for partying was attractive to Milo, he was broke all the time and couldn't afford it. He was being paid $50 per month, but his company commander ordered each of his men to buy a $50.00 war bond from his wages, which cost $37.50. He also had to buy $10 ticket books to shop at the PX (the Post Exchange—a general store on base run by the Army). His laundry cost him about $7 a month. All this added up to more than he made. There was nothing left to pay for leaves.

Instead, Milo volunteered to take other men's weekend guard duty, for which he charged ten dollars (around $147 in today's money) He also made $5 to $10 a week "fixing" other recruits' web belts, leggings, packs, belts, and rifle belts. Seasoned soldiers treated rookie GIs differently, showing them little respect. (The term GI was a nickname adopted by soldiers some years earlier; see GI in the Glossary for more information.) Veteran soldiers knew who newcomers were by the color and cleanliness of those belts and equipment. Recruits paid Milo to wash the items with harsh army soap so they looked well worn. With all that work, Milo eventually had some money but little time for weekends off. The first instance when he had a pass and enough cash, he made his way to Jacksonville. The bus to town, which cost fifty cents, drove through the camp and stopped at various locations to pick up soldiers. After the last stop, it proceeded to the double front gates, one for vehicles and one for personnel. The trainees had to get off the bus and see the first sergeant at the pedestrian gate. While they stood in line to get their passes signed, the empty bus drove through the vehicle gate and waited. The men walked through the pedestrian gate, showed their passes to an MP, and re-boarded the bus.

The first thing Milo did when he got to Jacksonville that day was to get in a poker game at the USO and lose all his money. He didn't even have the fifty cents needed for the bus ride back to base. He walked the streets for a while, but there wasn't much to see—except servicemen. Over 100,000 Army troops were stationed at Camp Blanding, and Jacksonville was a favorite spot for their leaves. There were also sailors and marines from a nearby naval air station and a marine base, more of them than there were soldiers from Camp Blanding. Almost every male he saw was in uniform.

He went back to the USO, had free coffee and doughnuts for dinner, and stayed over Saturday night in a free upper bunk. By the next day, he was fed up with coffee and doughnuts when he heard somebody ask, "Who wants a free meal?" Milo jumped up and said he did. They told him he'd have to go to a church to get it, which was not very appealing to him; he envisioned having to attend a religious service and sing hymns. Though not pleased at the prospect, his desire to eat overcame his qualms, and he boarded a half-empty bus that took him to the church. He was surprised to discover the meal was being served in a basement recreation room filled with about 200 good-looking young women, and attending a service wasn't required. He was quite pleased.

Besides having a filling meal, he met an attractive, charming young woman. The two spent the rest of the day together until Milo had to return to base. His new friend solved his financial predicament by giving him the fifty cents needed for the bus ride back to camp. After that weekend, the bus would bring men to the front gates, just as before. Everybody got off, went through the personnel gate, and got back on the bus. Everyone, that is, except Milo. He would walk over to a large LaSalle with gasoline ration stickers all over the windows and a dazzling blond at the wheel. Not only did Milo consider the girl's companionship an incredible blessing, but those ration stickers were an added gift. Only someone with a lot of importance could get them, and her father was well-to-do and influential: the editor and publisher of one of the local newspapers. The stickers meant the couple could buy all the gas they needed and be able to drive almost anywhere, something impossible for most American citizens. Milo considered his life was charmed while he was at Camp Blanding. He eventually had to leave, of course, but he did return to St. Augustine to visit the young lady once more.

Boot camp had involved plenty of orders and strictness, lots of night training, and quite a bit of yelling at the recruits. But Milo had already been the target of a lot of hollering by his superiors before he started Basic, so that didn't faze him. He thought the way the cadets had been treated was fair; there wasn't any hazing, and he was never rousted out of bed at night for a forced march or calisthenics. He also rated the military training he received at Camp Blanding as excellent. Even so, aside from the times he had with his girlfriend, he hated Basic Training, and couldn't wait for it to be over. Finally, after seventeen long weeks, it was.

Chapter 3

Over There

M ilo's ASTP status again had the Army confused. Since the program no longer existed, they didn't know where to send him, so he stayed at Camp Blanding—more or less alone. The training cadre was still there, as well as thousands of cadets. But there was no one from his company, which had shipped out. He later heard they were sent to Italy and almost all were wiped out at the Rapida River Crossing near Anzio, part of the Monte Cassino campaign.[1] In retrospect, it would seem the Army's confusion over Milo's future was a blessing in disguise, but Milo didn't know that at the time. He was stranded again, frustrated, and fed up with the work details they were giving him. He hid out when he could to avoid them, but still wound up with plenty.

First, the training cadre offered him a post as a "dog robber," the term given to an officer's orderly. Dog robbers shined their officer's shoes, made his bed, and acted more or less as a valet. The officers were usually just as tired as the trainees and appreciated whatever help they could get. Milo was insulted when he was offered the job. He considered himself every bit as good as any of the officers. He didn't want to have to clean up their beer bottles and ashtrays. The officers told him this was just about the best job in the Army for an enlisted man. There was little to do, and what there was, was easy. That didn't ease Milo's indignation, and he declined the post.

The dog robber offer was withdrawn and, with his dignity intact, Milo was ordered to the officer's mess (dining hall) as permanent KP (kitchen police). Not only that, but he was assigned to the grease detail: he had to clean out slimy sinks and filthy grease traps. It was a revolting, stinky job. He was staying in an NCO trainers' barracks and he smelled so bad the other men made him take showers with all his clothes on. Thankfully, that assignment lasted only a couple of weeks. Along the way he came to realize the officers trying to make him a dog robber were right. It was just about the best duty in the Army. Probably all he'd have to do was make the officer's bed. He likely cursed his pride after that.

Other jobs followed the KP assignment. Someone needed help at the motor pool and Milo was assigned. He had to move huge trucks around the area but didn't know how to drive them. Nobody told him the transmissions had to be double-clutched to switch gears, and he wound up driving for miles in first gear. After that, he was appointed a lifeguard at the nurses' beach. That sounded to him like great duty, but turned out not to be. All the nurses were working, and nobody was there but him. The job lasted only three or four days. He also filled in as a bugler at Battalion HQ several times.

One day he was assigned to the mess sergeant in the officers' mess, a man called the Duke of Fontana. He came from Fontana, California, but Milo never figured out why he was called the duke. The man was in charge of both the officer's mess and the mess for enlisted personnel; officers ate alone and did not mingle with non-officers. The enlisted men's mess was not fancy. Furniture and furnishings were spartan and military. The Army furnished the meals, and the men had no choice of dishes. Whatever the cooks made that day was what the GIs ate. Officers, on the other hand, paid for their meals and had a mess more like a nice restaurant, with proper dining tables, china, and silverware. Officers were also offered a choice of two entrées . One was the same as what the enlisted men were being served that day, but to hide that reality, the mess sergeant gave the dish a more upscale name. What GIs received as stew, for instance, was called "Braised Tenderloin Tips" in the officers' mess. Milo's duties included helping to make up fancy names for the food and writing the choices of the day on a blackboard near the door. Like all KP workers, he mopped floors, filled sugar and salt and pepper containers, and made sure the mess hall was neat and clean. He also peeled potatoes, the task historically associated with and complained about by soldiers assigned to KP. Contrary to the usual GI attitude, Milo thought it was the best KP job he could get. He stood at a window right across from the PX and could watch girls going in and out as he worked.

The Duke of Fontana was an avid ping-pong fan and liked to play between and after mess duties. He found out Milo could play, wanted him available as an opponent, and so appointed him Dining Room Orderly (DRO). Dressed in a white coat, Pvt. Flaten stood by the door, greeted the officers, and answered questions they had about the meal. When mess officers came in to inspect, he yelled "Attention." Mess halls were inspected often and carefully, as the Army didn't want diseases breaking out among its troops. He was also instructed that when the mess sergeant entered the room, he was to call out, "Here comes the Duke of Fontana."

As DRO, he had another duty which had little to do with mess halls: monitoring the local dog population. There were dogs all around the camp; every company had three or four. Milo had no idea how they got there, but whenever they engaged in breeding and got stuck, as dogs will, it was his job to pour cold water on them to get them to separate. And he had another dog-related duty: each day he'd collect two dollars from the mess sergeant and each man on KP. After work he'd take a bus to the dog track at Jacksonville. His mission there was to place bets on the dog races on behalf of the KP staff. The bus he caught on the way back dropped him off at 11:00 p.m. Since he had to be up at five, he was almost always tired.

Someone in command finally decided Milo's future lay elsewhere, and one day he was ordered to get all his gear together. "You're getting on a troop train," the sergeant said. Milo knew what that meant. There was a troop train leaving camp every day, and all the soldiers on board went to the same place: Replacement Depot

No. 1 at Fort Meade, Maryland, located about 35 miles northeast of Washington, D.C. Repple depples, as most GIs called them (though some said "repo depos"), were camps where troops were temporarily assigned and held until they were sent to permanent assignments. Most soldiers stayed at Ft. Meade a week or two and then shipped out to Europe. That's what was planned for Milo, but his experience was to be a little different—as were most of his Army experiences to date.

Though the depot was a holding facility, the Army didn't let up on training. There was lots of PT, drilling, and classes, but the men did get weekend leaves. While Milo was there, an old girlfriend from Minneapolis was in the area visiting her brother, a cadet at the Naval Academy in Annapolis. She asked Milo to take her to a fancy party at the Mayflower Hotel in Washington, D.C., which he was happy to do. When the party ended, he took his date back to her quarters and then had to get right back to Fort Meade. Training exercises in flamethrower operations were scheduled for early the next morning. Milo boarded a bus headed for the base, climbed into a luggage rack, and promptly fell asleep. The bus driver never saw him there. After discharging what he thought were his last passengers at Ft. Meade, he drove the bus back to the company garage in Laurel, MD, about ten miles away. By the time Milo got a ride back to the Fort, it was morning and his unit was already lined up, preparing to march out for the flamethrower drill.

When Milo walked up to the group still clad in his dress uniform and shoes, the sergeant in charge chewed him out thoroughly for being late and in the wrong uniform. He made Milo pick up a rifle and a flamethrower, march the distance to the practice field, practice with the weapon, and march back to his barracks. A flamethrower has two parts: a backpack containing canisters of liquid fuel and propellant, and a gun that propels the burning liquid. Together they weigh about seventy pounds. With his M1 rifle adding nine pounds, Milo put a lot of extra weight on dress shoes not made for marching, resulting in a blister on his foot.

After almost a month at Fort Meade, Milo and his sore foot were sent to Camp Kilmer, at New Brunswick, NJ, about 30 miles southwest of New York City. This was a staging area where troops were quartered until being shipped over to Europe. One day Milo thought he heard familiar voices in the barracks. He checked it out, and there were his old friends, Marco DeSantis and Danny Rinaldi. They had just been released from an Army penal colony, and like Milo, were being sent overseas as replacements.

Milo stayed at Camp Kilmer almost a month before he was told he was about to be shipped out, but where or when he'd be going wasn't revealed. The Army was being extremely secretive, fearing the Germans would learn its plans for the upcoming invasion. There were warnings posted all around telling everyone to keep their lips sealed: "Tell no one what you might know." "Loose lips sink ships" was another of the favored slogans. On one of his weekends at Kilmer, Milo got a pass and visited New York City. Taxi drivers there were used to GI fares, most of them being young, rather naïve boys. The cabbies liked to make up stories and tell the young soldiers all sorts of silliness just to amuse themselves. Milo recognized it for what it was and laughed it off, but then one driver told him, among a bunch of nonsensical things, that he'd be going overseas next week on the Queen Mary. He wondered whether the driver could possibly be right, but given the man's other foolishness, seriously doubted it. As it turned out, the driver was right. Or, should have been right. The Queen Mary sailed for Scotland the next week, just as the cabbie had predicted. Milo was scheduled to be on it— but wasn't. The blister on his foot became infected, which led to blood poisoning, and he was admitted to the camp's hospital and treated for three days. Mindful of the cab driver's prediction, Milo thought the Army's attempts at secrecy weren't very successful.

He was sufficiently healed by April 17th and boarded the Queen Elizabeth, also headed for Scotland. The RMS Queen Elizabeth was a luxury liner built in 1940 by the Cunard White Star Line. Along with her sister ship, the RMS Queen Mary, she was immediately pressed into service as a troop transport.[2] She was 1,031 feet long with a beam (width) of 118 feet. As a peacetime cruise ship, the liner was designed to carry a maximum of 2,283 passengers, plus a crew of more than a thousand. When used as a troop transport she could hold 12,000 to 14,000 troops. Both Queens were fast, capable of maintaining speeds of 28 knots. No known warships could keep up with them, so they each sailed alone, without a protective convoy. Fast or not, though, the ships zig-zagged all the way across the Atlantic so any submarine that might chance upon them wouldn't have a clear shot. The turns the ship made at that speed were steep. Men and their belongings were tossed about from side to side every seven or eight minutes. Quite a few GIs incurred their first WWII injuries as a result.

The vessel was triple-loaded. Every usable square inch of space was occupied. Milo was assigned to a stateroom on a lower deck that was filled with racks of canvas bunks built three high. His bunk was one of two built over the bathtub. There were also bunks built into the companionways (halls). Not much fresh air reached these lower areas, so groups of men were rotated, with each spending ten hours on the upper promenade deck before returning to their sleeping quarters. Getting fed was a competitive effort; Milo complained it took a mind like a steel trap to get any food. Though the trip took five days, DeSantis and Rinaldi were on board, and Milo enjoyed their friendly companionship and the benefit of their street smarts. While they may not have been highly educated, they knew a lot about practical things Milo didn't. They showed him the ropes and kept him safe. Milo was also a beneficiary of the men's gambling abilities, as they shared with him some of the money they won in crap games.

When the ship approached Scotland, it was met by a convoy of English warships, which accompanied it the last hundred miles. The liner sailed north up the Firth of Clyde on the west side of Scotland and dropped anchor offshore at Greenock, a town about 20 miles northwest of Glasgow. It was cold and raining, and the troops had to go ashore in open barges, a disagreeable welcome to the British Isles. Milo was assigned to a packet headed for the 29th Division Replacement Battalion (packets were groups of men who might be from various units temporarily assigned to travel together to the same location.) It struck Milo as odd that the 29th was getting replacements even though it hadn't yet seen combat. He soon discovered the need resulted from the many injuries caused by the intensive training the men were getting.

Milo's packet was headed for Cornwall in the southwest corner of England, more than 500 miles away. The group boarded a rickety troop train which traveled most of two days to get there. The GIs had to sleep on slats covered by straw mattresses. Milo didn't enjoy the trip. Their destination was Camp Tavistock, a former British Army post located only a mile from the edge of a huge moor called Dartmoor. Tavistock was old and not very comfortable. Still, it was preferable to the many pre-invasion camps scattered around England where men were living in tents—and far superior to those he would encounter in the months to come.

Milo's locations late April, 1944, to D-Day (June 6, 1944)

Chapter 4

Try, Try Again

Milo's new division, the 29th Infantry, had an interesting history. It came into existence during World War I and, like other infantry divisions, contained three infantry regiments: the 115th, 116th, and 175th Infantries. The companies comprising those regiments were National Guard units from the District of Columbia and towns in Virginia and Maryland. A number of those companies had fought in the Revolutionary War, and many had been in the Civil War. Some had fought for the North and others for the South. There was a concern that former Union units might be opposed to serving with those that had been Confederate, and vice versa. As things turned out, the men got along just fine. A shoulder patch for the division was designed to honor its history. It resembled the Asian symbol for yin and yang: half was blue and the other half gray. The 29th became known as The Blue and Gray Division.

The government federalized the 29th's National Guard units in October 1940 and ordered their members to report for duty in February 1941. After training stateside for twenty months, the division shipped out to England and continued its rigorous training as soon as it settled into camp. The strenuous maneuvers were still going strong when Milo arrived. He didn't know why, of course, but part of his division was being prepared for a starring role in the coming invasion of Europe.

The 29th's senior officers were all Regular Army, not National Guard or Army Reserve, and many had graduated from West Point. They considered themselves the elite of the officer corps and looked on Guard and Reserve officers as being second class. They felt far superior to what they considered the raggedy groups of citizen-soldiers being placed under their command. With that prejudice, most invasion planners were against using an untried National Guard division in the initial assault on France. They presumed Guard units were incapable of fighting as effectively as Regular Army units.

In 1943 the 29th got a new Commanding General, Major General Charles Gerhardt. He was flamboyant, a strict disciplinarian, and an avid career soldier. He decided he could train the men under him to be equal to any Regular Army outfit, more than capable of taking the lead in the coming invasion. To that end, he further intensified the division's already tough training.

When Milo arrived, most of what the men were doing was field marching long distances in the nearby moor, always wearing full backpacks and their steel helmets. A moor is a large wasteland, barren of everything but grass and low vegetation. Dartmoor, where Milo was in training, covers 954 square miles and is near both the cities of Tavistock and Plymouth. True to English weather's reputation, there was almost always rain and fog on the moor. Winds were so constant and vigorous that hardly anything grew above ground level. It was a miserable, cold, wet place to be, but in many ways an ideal Army training ground. Its uninhabited vastness allowed for many different exercises to be practiced simultaneously. The men could fire live ammunition and explosives from various weapons without endangering people or nearby populated areas. They could practice battle strategies such as fire and maneuver, at will. The drills were undoubtedly valuable, but to Milo, it was the same old stuff he'd had in basic training. Again, he was bored.

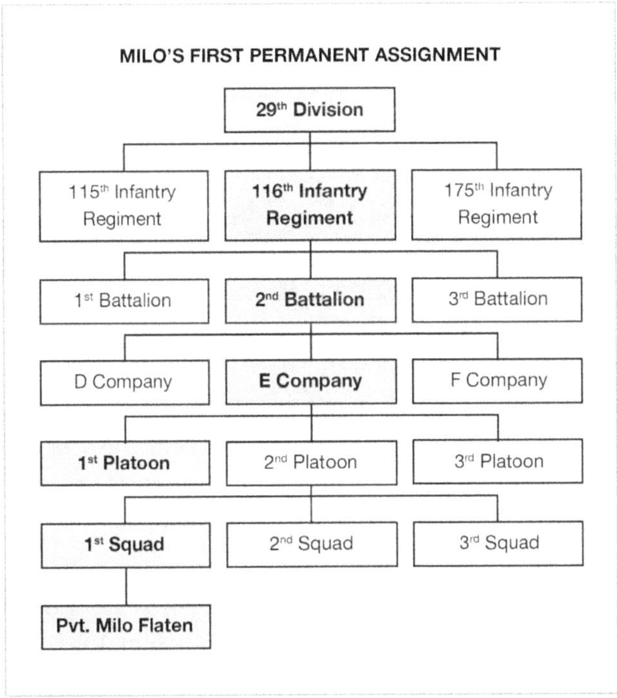

In May Milo was permanently assigned to the First Squad, First Platoon, E Company, 2nd Battalion, 116th Infantry Regiment, 29th Inf. Division. The 116th was a storied regiment: it began as the Virginia Colonial militia in 1760 and fought in the Revolutionary War. In the Civil War, it was the Confederacy's 2nd Virginia Regiment, commanded by Gen. Thomas Jackson. At the First Battle of Manassas (also called the First Battle of Bull Run) the 2nd Virginia came under intense fire. General Jackson stood boldly out in the open, watching and directing his troops. A fellow general yelled, "There stands Jackson, like a stone wall." That phrase became the nickname of both the general and Milo's regiment; the 116th was called The Stonewallers.

E Company was an Army National Guard unit from Chase City, Virginia, a little rural town on the southern border of Virginia, about 160 miles west of Norfolk. Guard units from similar towns made up the regiment's other companies.[1] Milo felt the men he was with in E Company were much the same as his colleagues in basic training.

They were mostly rural southerners with thick accents, and unintelligent or not, he considered them so. He had one buddy he got along well with, a New York native from a different platoon named Bob Hirsch.[2] Although Hirsch probably had a typical New Yorker's accent, his speech was much closer to Milo's than the southern boys'. He was athletic and as tall as Milo. Milo thought him highly intelligent and believed he was the strongest man he'd ever met. The two became good friends.

As noted, the Commanding General of the 29th Division, Maj. Gen. Gerhardt, was a strict, by-the-book veteran of World War I. He was very tough on his soldiers, a stickler for discipline, and wanted his men to fear him. One of his standing orders was that all soldiers in the 29th had to wear their helmet's chinstrap at all times. Although Army manuals mandated this practice, no other unit commanders required it of their men. Gerhardt became known for this and got the nickname Chinstrap Charlie. In fact, the 29th was dubbed the Chinstrap Division. The general wanted his men always ready, always energetic, and always going forward. While they were training, he would yell at them, "Twenty-nine, let's go." Soon that became the division's motto. As time went on, the general insisted his men had to accompany everything they did with yells of "Twenty-nine, let's go!"

The Army's 1st Division (nicknamed "The Big Red One") was also in England, only about ten miles away from the 29th. It, too, was busy training for the amphibious assault that would soon take place. Only the invasion planners and highly ranked officers knew it at the time, but the Allies planned to attach Milo's 116th Regiment to the 1st Division, and this joint force was to be part of the first wave of troops in the invasion. (The 115th and 175th Regiments would follow in later waves.) The 1st Division was Regular Army, and its men were experienced in warfare, having been in heavy combat in Italy. They were battle weary, combat wise, and had lost whatever innocence they might have had as recruits. They weren't interested in looking sharp or obeying weird orders. The 29th, on the other hand, had never seen combat, and with its chinstrap requirement, clean, sharp uniforms, and strict discipline, probably appeared pretty comical to 1st Division vets. But General Gerhardt was determined to make his National Guard soldiers just as good as any regular Army troops. He wanted them to believe they were the best soldiers around, convinced they could beat the Germans. Milo realized after a while, to his surprise, that such an attitude really did prevail. The men of the 29th had come to believe themselves unbeatable.

After Milo joined E Company, his training was no longer a boring repetition of things he'd learned in boot camp. It now concentrated on specific aspects of the invasion his unit would encounter. The company traveled by railroad to the Army's Assault Training Center at Slapton Sands, a coastal area near Plymouth where the beach was similar to Normandy's. Gun emplacements like those the Germans had on the French coast had been constructed on the shore. The men repeatedly practiced landings and fire and maneuver to get a feel for what they'd face. The drills went on for hours. It seemed to Milo he attacked one particular pillbox at least sixty times. They went to another location and climbed down Jacob's Ladders, the rope netting used to transfer men from a large ship to a small landing craft. One of the more important things they learned was to keep their hands on the vertical ropes as they descended. If they forgot and used the horizontal lines, the man coming down from above might stomp on their fingers. This exercise, while valuable, was practiced on a thirty-foot wall on dry land, and in no way simulated the movement of ships in rolling seas.

E company then went to a local school with a heated swimming pool for Mae West training. A Mae West was the inflatable life jacket issued by the military, named in honor of the blond, buxom Broadway and movie star of the day. When the men got in the water, Milo was startled to see that most of them didn't swim well — or at all. Only he and Hirsch were experienced swimmers. Hirsch had spent his boyhood summers in the ocean at his parents' beach-front vacation home on Long Island. He was as skilled a swimmer as Milo.

They were next introduced to the LCVP, which stood for

"Landing Craft Vehicle, Personnel," a small boat that carried attacking infantrymen ashore during invasions from the sea.[3] They were also called Higgins boats, after the man who designed and built them. When the Army started planning the invasion of Europe, it realized it would need thousands of small boats to ferry troops across the English Channel and discharge them onto the beach. At the time there wasn't any existing craft that could fill the bill. Andrew Higgins was building small wooden boats in New Orleans for the oil exploration industry. Once the war started, he lobbied hard and convincingly that he could supply the needed landing craft, and was awarded a contract. The flat-bottomed boats he designed were thirty-six feet long, ten feet wide, and made of plywood with quarter-inch armor plating on the sides. The bow was a steel ramp which could be raised and lowered. Ideally the boat would beach itself on the shore, the ramp would be lowered, and soldiers could quickly run onto dry land. Each boat could hold up to thirty-six men plus a crew of four, though frequently only thirty or thirty-one soldiers were boarded because of all the cumbersome equipment they carried. The craft's 225-horsepower engine could propel it to a top speed of about twelve knots when empty, but only nine when fully loaded. They were armed with two .30 caliber machine guns mounted in the stern. GIs were told the boats would be manned by Coast Guard or Navy crews that were experienced in amphibious invasions.

Six or seven LCVPs were needed to carry each company to shore. The men were divided into boat groups, with each man having a specific assignment. Some, like Milo, were riflemen, while others were engineers and demolition experts. The latter were to clear tank traps and other German obstacles, creating two open lanes to the beach so men and machines landing later would have a clear path. Still others were assigned to direct traffic or handle medical problems. Each boat group was loaded onto its LCVP in a well-planned sequence so the men could get off in the order it was assumed they'd be needed. Riflemen would be first.

Over time, the troops were moved into areas which provided opportunities for specialized training. Milo's company spent time in three towns: Torquay, on the channel's coast just a few miles from Dartmoor; Newquay, across the peninsula, on the opposite, west coast of Cornwall; and Land's End, at the very western tip of the Cornwall peninsula. He felt all three were uncomfortably close to German lines, only about 85 miles across the English Channel. Land's End struck him as particularly vulnerable, and when he drew guard duty there on pitch-dark nights, he was quite scared.

Soldiers stayed two to a dwelling in private homes which had been confiscated from their owners. Many of the GIs were teenagers, just out of high school, and until now, sometimes acted foolishly, as teenagers will. If there was a chance to pull a prank or goof off, they'd take it. But Milo noticed the closer they got to combat, the young men became more considerate. They acted maturely and responsibly in the borrowed homes and were careful not to harm the owners' property. Milo was surprised, but guessed the importance of what they were about to do inspired them to decide to grow up. Many of the owners came back to their houses on weekends and stayed with the soldiers. They always thanked the GIs for being in England and in their homes. They'd borne the brunt and hardships of the war by themselves for years and, despite having their country overrun by Yanks, were immensely grateful America had joined them to fight the Nazis. Many British soldiers (nicknamed Tommies) resented American troops because they were paid more, had more luxuries (such as the amount of toilet paper issued to each man, if that can be termed a luxury), and seemed to be more attractive to English girls. (Their catch-phrase for GIs was "Overpaid, oversexed, and over here.") But Milo observed that most civilian Brits and American soldiers acted kindly and respectfully to each other.

In mid-May E Company was taken to one of many marshaling areas near Southampton, a good-sized port city about six miles north of the English Channel coast on a large connecting waterway called Southampton Water. It was an ideal area to store many of the ships that were to take part in the coming invasion.

The troops called these holding areas sausages because that's what they looked like on aerial photos and maps. They were large expanses of bare land enclosed by chain link fencing with barbed wire on top. Once penned in, the GIs couldn't leave; security was extremely tight. MPs guarded the enclosures, and men from Intelligence roamed around, listening for talk that might contain something useful to the Germans. The Allies knew Germany was expecting an invasion, and were doing their best to make sure the enemy wouldn't find out when or where it was to take place. In fact, they were making quite an effort to convince Germans that the attack would come at Pas de Calais, the point of land in France nearest to England, quite some distance from the intended landing sites.

There were no barracks in the sausages; the men lived in tents, and most of their time was taken up with close order drill, just to keep them occupied. The GIs were aware they'd soon invade France and there would be heavy casualties. All of them were apprehensive; many expected to die. Yet Milo sensed most of them weren't really scared at that point.

The monotony of constant marching finally got to Milo. His company was looking for people to volunteer for certain necessary jobs. To get out of drill, he told a sergeant he was a barber (he wasn't, by any means). They gave him hand-operated shears and an orange crate and told him to start giving haircuts. He naively assumed there wouldn't be anything to it, but after cutting one man's hair he realized the result looked terrible. He said to the soldier, "You don't want to look like that, do you?" The man said no, so Milo cut off all his hair. GIs standing around watching thought it was all very funny. The CO happened by, saw Milo's handiwork, and didn't consider it humorous at all. He ordered the shorn soldier to cut all of Milo's hair off, too.[4] This somewhat insignificant incident would soon be of some importance to Milo.

While the men were held in the sausages, they were completely in the dark about invasion plans; in fact, only about 200 ranking officers knew them. The remaining officers and non-coms were finally told, and on May 28th they briefed the rest of the troops. Allied soldiers were going to invade France at five locations on the Normandy shore at beaches code-named Sword, Juno, Gold, Utah and Omaha. The invasion was code-named Operation Overlord, and was led by the Supreme Allied Commander, US General Dwight D. Eisenhower. Americans would land on Utah and Omaha, with British and Canadians hitting the other beaches. The 116th Regiment was attached to the 1st Division for the assault. The 1st Division would lead the invasion on the eastern half of Omaha Beach, while the initial landing on the western half would be made by the 116th, led by companies A, E, F, and G. Milo's E Company was to be the first to storm the beach in its sector.

Once the men knew the plans, training was specific to the area where each group was to land. The men were shown rubber mockups of their landing areas displaying its buildings, gun emplacements, and other landmarks. They were told to memorize the model as they'd need to know their location at all times. Officers and some NCOs were issued maps of the invasion area, but they were printed in French and no one in Milo's company could read them—except Milo. He volunteered to his CO that he'd studied French in high school and would be willing to help with the maps. He was immediately appointed the company's 1st scout and given a set of maps to take with him. In that role, he'd be first to hit the beach. While this assignment was extremely dangerous and might have triggered anger or resentment, Milo took it without ill will. He was used to doing as he was told. Besides, the captain told him, "Just think, Flaten, you'll be leading eight million men across Europe into the heart of Berlin. You'll be a hero." Both Milo and the captain laughed and thought that was quite funny. Neither could imagine how close the statement might be to the truth.

Chapter 5

The Bounding Main

After three weeks of confinement in the sausage, the GIs were taken to their ships in the dark of night on June 4, 1944. Milo's company boarded the USS Thomas Jefferson, a two-year-old troop transport designed to carry 1260 troops and a crew of 593. It was 492 feet long and 70 feet wide and carried thirty LCVPs hung on its sides by marine cranes called davits. Invasion plans called for the ship and others like it to carry men and their landing craft most of the way across the English Channel via a lane marked by small patrol boats. About eleven miles from the French coast the Jefferson would stop, and GIs would transfer to the Higgins boats, which would carry them the rest of the way to shore. They were to hit the beach at 6:30 a.m. on the morning of June 5th. Milo's LCVP was to be the first one to go in, leading the charge, and he, as 1ˢᵗ scout, was to be first man off the boat, leading the others in.

The Jefferson left its dock and started for an assembly area in the Channel near the Isle of Wight, where it, and the other ships around it, pitched and rolled in the high seas. Conditions were terrible: winds were high, it was foggy, there was constant heavy rain, and seas were roiling. The invasion planners were well aware an amphibious assault requires calm to moderate seas and decent visibility to succeed, and the Allied meteorologists were predicting extremely bad weather all the next day. Based on those forecasts, General Eisenhower decided to postpone the invasion. Some ships had not yet left port, and those that had put out to sea returned. The Thomas Jefferson, which had sailed out far enough to be in sight of the French coast, headed back toward England and remained underway without docking.

The troops buried in the Jefferson's lower decks had no idea what was happening. They were not told the invasion had been postponed or that General Eisenhower and his staff had met again late at night on the 4th and reviewed updated weather information. New forecasts showed the storm would soon abate, leaving a small window of opportunity. After much debate and deliberation Eisenhower concluded that the weather, though still marginal, would improve enough to allow the invasion to proceed on the morning of the sixth. If he waited any longer, the next time conditions for the assault would be favorable might be weeks away.

The Jefferson's passengers stayed on board the rocking vessel all day on the fifth, and overnight into the morning of the sixth. They were crammed together below decks so tightly they could scarcely move without bumping into each other. The closeness was overwhelming. Milo kept to his bunk much of the time but got up every few hours and moved around as often as he could to stay limber. He had experienced crowding on the ship coming over to Britain, but this was far worse. The Jefferson heaved and rolled in the choppy sea. Not only was the journey miserable, but the soldiers were being kept in the dark while nervously contemplating their fate in the upcoming invasion. To add to their discomfort, the ship's engines roared loudly; by now the men had been listening to them for over thirty hours.

Suddenly a piercing bosun's whistle sounded over the PA, startling the jittery GIs. A voice ordered all naval personnel to their stations. A little later the engines stopped and there was silence. The absence of noise was a relief, but also unnerving. About 3:00 a.m. another bosun's whistle sounded, followed by the order for assault troops to move to their debarkation area. The men got their bulky gear together and shuffled to the upper deck.

Arriving topside, Milo found the weather still horrible, with heavy rain and a cold wind. The sky was overcast and he could barely make out the dim outlines of nearby ships. A Jacob's Ladder was draped over the rail, and his LCVP hung halfway down the side of the ship, suspended by lines attached to its davit. A sergeant held a quick roll call and ordered the first boat group to board. Milo and the other men clambered over the rail and stepped gingerly down the netting. When they had loaded, their little boat was jammed full. Only a few men could sit while the rest had to stand. Most of them preferred that; with all their gear, they could barely get up from a sitting position.

The troops were fully equipped for the invasion. Their uniform pants and shirts were made of heavy wool and worn over long underwear. The outer garments had been treated with chemicals to make them impervious to gas. Germany had used poison gas as a weapon in WWI, and the Allies were prepared in case they used it again. Though the precaution might have been safer for the GIs, it brought about an obnoxious situation: when the fabric got wet, it became clammy and sticky and gave off a sickening odor. Over those uniforms, the troops wore various straps, packs, tools, and equipment, plus bandoliers (belts) of ammunition. Along with their rifle, all their gear weighed about sixty pounds. Men with BARs, bazookas, and such, carried even heavier loads.

Once Milo's boat group was aboard, the ship's crew lowered their LCVP into the Channel. It descended in a near free-fall, hitting the water with a huge splash. Men were wildly tossed about and many fell, but they were packed in so tightly no one went overboard. As the coxswain revved the engine to full power, the little boat began to circle the Jefferson, with other boats joining the convoy as they launched. Within minutes, wind-driven rain and waves crashing over the rail had soaked the men to their skin, and the obnoxious odor of their uniforms filled the air. The landing craft began to take on water faster than its pumps could handle. The boat's crewmen told the GIs to bail it out with their helmets; some nearest the rail tried but made little headway.

The crew manning Milo's LCVP were Coast Guard Chief Petty Officers (CPOs), non-commissioned officers equivalent in rank to Army sergeants. Milo stood in the front by the ramp, next to the bowman who acted as a lookout and ramp operator. The other crewmen were in the stern, with the coxswain at the helm driving the vessel and the two gunners at their machine guns. Milo knew LCVPs had been used in earlier amphibious landings and had heard that the men operating them were experienced at invasions. He asked the bowman about it and the chief said he'd never done anything like this before. His prior job was operating a Lake Michigan lighthouse in Manitowoc, Wisconsin. So much for seasoned veterans, Milo thought.

It took about an hour to launch all the landing craft from the Jefferson. When the last one was in the water they formed into columns heading across the channel. Waves were huge and unrelenting. The vessels rose and fell and wallowed sideways at the same time. Most of the men became seasick. The Army had provided seasick pills, but those who had taken them in the past found they caused sleepiness. Many who wanted to stay alert when they hit the beach ignored the pills and wound up terribly ill. The floor of the boat became slippery with vomit and seawater sloshing back and forth. The smell, along with the odor from the uniforms, caused men who were otherwise all right to succumb. Milo was fortunate and never got sick, which he attributed to being preoccupied with leading the charge. He was too busy concentrating on what was happening and thinking about what he'd do when he landed.

While his boat had been circling, Milo was unable to see much, but once it headed towards shore dawn began to break. From the crest of a wave, he spied the shadowy forms of LCVPs nearby and noted his was ahead of them all, leading the V formation. As they plowed through the stormy seas his thoughts nervously alternated between "Why me? Why me?" and "Wouldn't my dad be proud!"

On the way over, the CPOs played music on their PA system,

phonograph records by the Glenn Miller Orchestra. It was astonishing that the needle stayed in its groove without skipping, given how brutally the boat was being tossed around. They played only two songs: *Don't Sit Under the Apple Tree*, and *In the Mood*, one after the other, over and over. The music was apparently somebody's idea of how to cheer the invaders up, but Milo thought it asinine. The constant noise plus the sounds of the boat's engine just added to his discomfort.

The men had been briefed that B-17 bombers would fly over and bomb the beach and German fortifications before they went ashore, so they kept looking up for airplanes. Bombs would not only knock out enemy soldiers and guns, but would create craters on the beach that incoming GIs could use for shelter. Milo never saw any bombers, which made him nervous. Around 5:00 o'clock the sky brightened a bit, and he could now see the battleships, cruisers, destroyers, and thousands of other warships following his little craft.

So far things had been quiet. No one was shooting at the incoming vessels, and guns on Allied ships were silent. Then, about 5:30 a.m., a German artillery battery on shore began firing. Most of the shells landed short, but a few hit near the battleship Arkansas, causing huge splashes. There was no Allied response, which surprised Milo. About twenty minutes later he saw yellow lights ahead in the water, which he learned were flares placed by the signal corps to guide the convoy. They were also signals to the warships. When the big vessels reached the lights, they started firing their huge guns at the beach. In a speech he made during training, Gen. Omar Bradley had told the men they'd have "ringside seats for the biggest show on earth." Once the big guns started firing Milo understood what the general meant. The battleships Texas and Arkansas, along with destroyers, cruisers, and other warships, all behind the LCVPs, fired salvo after salvo from their enormous cannons. Some shells were so big Milo could hear and even faintly see them overhead. Recoil created by the firing was strong enough to push the huge ships backward, causing enormous splashes. The sound was deafening, and fire from the guns and explosions on the beach lit up the murky sky like a gigantic fireworks display. The bombardment was to continue until the LCVPs reached the shore.

During this pandemonium, the Higgins craft sailed on, targeting on two small control boats about two-and-a-half miles offshore which marked the LD, or Line of Departure. The LCVPs were to form up there and start their final approach toward land at 6:13 a.m. When Milo's boat reached the LD, it was only 6:00 o'clock, so the landing craft lined up again and circled around, awaiting the departure time. The GIs onboard got a glimpse of Normandy and watched as British fighter planes patrolled the area. At 6:13 the boats formed into columns again and headed for shore. As they got closer, the men could see the beach was entirely flat. The bomb craters they had been expecting were not there. With no place to hide, they'd have to run across three hundred yards of flat, open sand with no cover. The bombers they'd been looking for had indeed flown over but were high above the cloud cover and the troops couldn't see or hear them. The clouds also prevented aircrews from seeing either the ground or their targets. Fearing their bombs might fall short onto the incoming Americans, the airmen delayed their drops. As a result, tons and tons of explosives fell harmlessly far inland, and not one bomb hit the beach or a German emplacement. And, unbelievably, all the shelling Milo witnessed from the warships behind him also went harmlessly over the beach and the German positions. The ship's gunners were also afraid of hitting the incoming landing vessels. It may have been the biggest show on earth, but it didn't do a thing to help the soldiers who were about to land there.

Invasion planners had divided Omaha beach into sectors designated by code names. The sector where Milo's boat group was to land was called Easy Green. The area abutting it to the east, where some boats from E Company were to land, was called Easy Red. The sector east of that was Fox Green, which was where the 16th Regiment, 1st Division, was to land. The 16th would also cover sectors farther to the east.

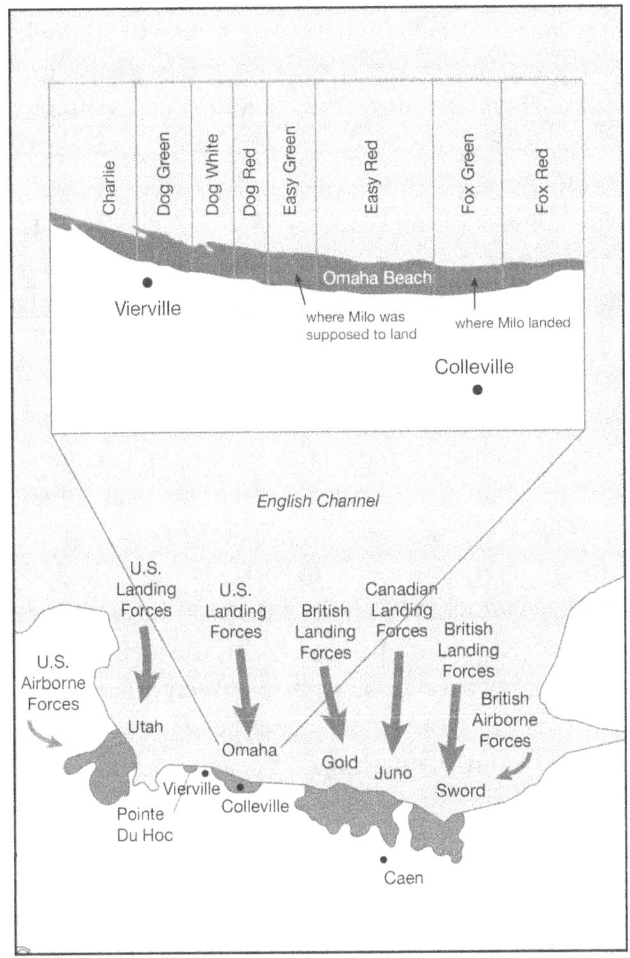

Omaha Beach locations

Several unexpected factors came into play as the landing craft neared shore. First, coxswains lost their bearings in the thick mist and smoke from the bombardment and were unable to see structures and formations that were to have guided them. Second, heavy winds were blowing from west to east. Third, a strong easterly current ran in the channel several miles offshore. These elements combined to cause many of the boats to come in far to the east of their intended targets. Two E Company boat crews did land where they were supposed to, and found their way to their assigned areas. The other

E Company vessels, including Milo's, were not as lucky. Milo's boat neared shore in the Fox Green zone designated for the 16th Regiment, 1st Division, more than a mile east of its target. As a result, the landscape and structures the men had memorized in England were now of little use. And instead of landing close together, his company was scattered over a long distance. Its officers and non-coms couldn't collect and lead their men, leaving young, inexperienced soldiers essentially on their own.

Milo figured his boat was about three hundred yards from the beach when it jarred to an abrupt stop. It might have run into one of the defensive devices planted by Germans, or it might have simply grounded on a sandbar. Whatever the case, Milo could now hear bullets pinging against the boat's metal ramp and armored sides. The Coast Guard crew started to lower the ramp as the PA announced, "Infantry, prepare to debark; the ramp is down." As it dropped in the water, German bullets that had been hitting the ramp now struck exposed men in the bow. Milo considered going over the side but couldn't because those behind pushed him forward. He ran off in a rush, as he would later describe it, "scooting out like a scared rabbit." He hit the water and at once started to sink. It was not a promising beginning for an invasion.

Chapter 6

Shock and Awe

Milo estimated the water was about fifteen feet deep. It was hard to tell because he descended very slowly. His helmet had trapped air and was making him somewhat buoyant. He tore off the helmet and liner, and then, calling on his Boy and Sea Scout training, raised his arms over his head and let everything loose slide off. He surfaced and went back under two or three times, all the while unbuckling and unsnapping his gear and shedding it. Finally, he was left with only his uniform and shoes. He tried to get the shoes off, but his leggins covered the laces, and he was unable to unstrap them in the rolling seas. He sank and surfaced again and found his rifle floating next to him. M1 Garands were composed of enough wood that they wouldn't sink. Milo grabbed the rifle and the sealed map container bobbing nearby and started swimming for the beach. Bullets whizzed around him and landed in the sea, making a "zip" sound and decelerating rapidly as they went into the water. He couldn't see them in the air, but he could follow their path after they hit. It dawned on him then that his bald, white head would be a perfect target for a kraut (one of the GIs' favorite derogatory names for Germans[1]). He knew he needed to find a helmet as soon as possible.

When he reached shallower water close to the beach, he took cover behind one of the German "hedgehog" tank traps. It was made of pieces of steel similar to railroad rails five or six feet long and welded together somewhat like lodge poles in a Native American teepee. The device gave him a little protection from bullets and shielded him somewhat from the Germans' view. He was utterly alone, hunched down in the shallow water, soaked through and as cold as he'd ever been. He was stunned and terrified; it felt as though the whole world was shooting at him.

Germans manned a large number of gun emplacements on the bluff that lay ahead. They were shooting rifles, machine guns, mortars, and artillery at him. They had long ago set up their weapons and sighted them in to cover as much of the beach as possible. Machine guns swept from one side to the other, intersecting at points and keeping a steady supply of lead almost everywhere on the sands. The volume of fire was astounding, and Milo well knew those people ahead were doing everything they could to kill him. At that moment he began to fully understand, perhaps for the first time, that he was totally expendable. He realized he was being sacrificed, sent to his death by his own country. All the propaganda he'd received during training—about fighting for freedom, saving your homeland, conquering a monstrous enemy—none of it was important now. He had to fight to live. He either killed or he would be killed. From this point on, his war was solely about survival. Any qualms he might have had about taking a life were quickly forgotten.

He stayed behind the hedgehog around forty-five minutes as corpses began floating in with the incoming tide. He watched as they washed up to the shore, those who had drowned and those who'd been blown up or shot. The dead men lined up like logs, parallel to the shoreline. Bodies and pieces of bodies were all around him as far as he could see, and the sea shone red in the scant morning light. It struck him he had never seen a dead body before, never even attended a funeral. He was petrified but did his best to concentrate on the instructions he'd received in England instead of the slaughter all around him. Yet he couldn't stop thinking he'd never survive this hell.

Mindful of his bare head, he set out among the dead in search of a helmet. It took a while as he was very particular. He didn't want one from a soldier who'd been shot in the head. After some rummaging around, he found a clean liner and helmet and collected ammunition and other items to replace what he'd lost in the sea. As he scavenged for gear, a few live soldiers came in close to him, mostly men from the 1st Division. One, however, was his pal, Bob Hirsch, who'd been part of a different E Company boat team. He trotted up to Milo carrying his BAR and said something like "Fancy meeting you here." Needless to say, he was a welcome sight.

The two men hid behind the hedgehog a little longer, working out a plan of sorts. They stood up and started running inland, first through shallow water and then across the hard sand of the beach. They knew how visible and vulnerable they were when running, so periodically they played dead, flopping down on their stomachs as if they'd been shot. After a few minutes, they'd jump up, run some more and drop again. Eventually, they made it across the three hundred yards of tidal flat to the shingle, the high water's edge. Others were doing the same thing, but most got hit. Milo and Hirsch made it in one piece.

The shingle, or seawall, was an area at the high-water line where small polished stones had washed up with the tides and, over a great span of time, piled up to form a shelf several yards wide. At most locations on the beach, it was two or three feet high, high enough for men to duck behind and evade small arms fire from ahead, but ineffective against the mortar and artillery fire raining down on them.

The random group of soldiers who congregated at the shingle was in a state of utter confusion and disorder. They were from Milo's regiment and the 1st Division, plus part of a Ranger unit that had also landed in the wrong place. Fifty to sixty men were gathered there, each hunkering down to hide from enemy fire, concentrating only on himself. No one was in command.

Beyond the seawall, there was a farm-type fence, a small ditch, and then a cobblestone road running parallel to the shoreline. Fifty or more yards beyond the road, the bluff rose at a sharp angle. The men had been told they were to scale it, assemble on top, and then head west towards the town of Vierville. At the moment, it didn't look to Milo as though that was going to happen. Besides the intense fire being laid down by the Germans, there was another obstacle to their reaching the cliff. The Germans had placed razor-sharp concertina wire on the far side of the cobblestone road, and signs hanging from the wire said "Achtung. Minen." (Attention. Mines.) Milo and Hirsch talked it over and decided to ignore the signs. They assumed the wire manufacturer had probably attached them to the wire before it was shipped to the front. They guessed there probably weren't any mines there, but the concertina wire was another matter which would have to be dealt with. Hirsch told Milo he'd get a Bangalore torpedo to blow a hole in the wire and moved off to find one.

Briefers in England had said there'd likely be a German counterattack soon after they landed, and that inspired Milo to take charge. He yelled at the GIs they would have to go. If they didn't make a run for it they'd certainly die on the beach. He said they might as well risk leaving their cover, as going forward would give them some breathing room if a counterattack did occur. He indicated he and Hirsch were going to blow the concertina wire, and they should get ready to move out. He told them to make sure everyone had a rifle, ammunition, and whatever other supplies and equipment they could scrounge from the dead.

At that moment, a 2nd lieutenant from the 1st Division showed up. He was crying and moaning, "Oh my God. Oh my God, this is terrible," and made no effort to take command. Milo was disgusted with the man.

Hirsch returned with a torpedo, but didn't know how to fire it. The crying lieutenant showed him how, and Hirsch climbed through the farm fence and ditch to reach the road. He ran across it in the face of heavy rifle fire and inserted the Bangalore into the mass of razor wire. He was just about to fire it when a bullet struck him in the forehead. Milo saw it hit—it was a tracer from a machine gun.

Every third bullet in a belt of machine gun ammo, both German and American, was coated with a chemical that glowed red after it was fired. To the machine gunner, it made the stream of bullets coming out of the barrel look like a laser beam. He was better able to aim his weapon knowing where it was pointed. To Milo, it allowed him to see the unthinkable.

Hirsch gave a little yell and toppled over onto the torpedo. Milo was concerned Hirsch might have already fired the weapon, and it was a hang fire, a delayed explosion. He told the guys around him to wait awhile to make sure it was safe. He also told them he didn't know how to fire the Bangalore as he'd never been trained on them.

After a few minutes, the lieutenant stopped crying, crawled up to the lane, and ran across it. Bullets hit the road all around him, causing sparks to fly off the cobblestones wherever they landed. The officer made it to Hirsch's body, pushed it aside, and checked to see if he was alive. Finding he wasn't, the officer pulled the cord which fired the torpedo and ran back across the road. Seconds later the device exploded, not only blowing a hole in the barbed wire but mangling Hirsch's body. Milo was impressed the lieutenant had shown so much courage, but the bravery was short-lived. The officer never stopped when he reached the seawall and kept right on running past the men toward the sea. Milo never saw him again.

Milo yelled, "Let's go," ran across the road, through the break in the barbed wire, and jumped into a German zig-zag trench. He checked and saw the other men were following him. Briefers had also said these defenses would be manned by Russian or Romanian troops, prisoners of war forced by the Nazis to serve in the German army. They wouldn't be fanatical about fighting and might well surrender. Milo looked around in the trench and found a German newspaper wrapped around part of a sandwich. He knew then it was Germans they were facing, not sympathetic POWs.

An American sailor appeared among the GIs. He said he was a forward observer (FO) from a destroyer assigned to the 1st Division's 16th Regiment. The man wore navy fatigues and the wide helmet used by naval personnel that allowed it to be worn over headphones. He had lost his radio but was carrying a shuttered lightbox, a device used to transmit coded messages using flashes of light. He stayed close to Milo and started pestering him with questions. Milo was annoyed but realized it was probably because he had been giving orders like he was a big shot. The sailor assumed he had rank.

The destroyer the FO came from had been shooting onto the beach, and now its shells were coming increasingly closer to Milo and his group. Milo told the observer to signal the destroyer to stop, that it was shooting at Americans. The man tried to use the lightbox, but it no longer worked. He pulled out a set of semaphore flags, stood up, and wig-wagged a message to the ship. There was a pause in the firing, and then a response flashed back which the observer translated: "Give yourselves up to the nearest Americans." The FO sent back, "We are Americans," but the ship started firing towards them again, not only HE (high explosives) but WP (white phosphorous) as well.

With both Americans and Germans shooting at them, it was clear Milo's group would have to do something if they wanted to survive. The area was becoming very dark due to the great deal of smoke generated by exploding WP rounds. Bursting shells had also set beach grasses on fire, adding to the thick smog. The smoke was so acrid the men couldn't stop coughing, but while the foul air was terrible to breathe, it kept the Germans from seeing them clearly.

Again, Milo took charge. Nobody challenged him or asked what a buck private was doing commanding a company-sized unit. He yelled to the men to put on their gas masks and climb the hill. They followed his orders and began the ascent. The bluff was steep there, an almost vertical cliff, and scaling it was difficult and tiring. They slung their rifles on their backs and used both hands to grab vegetation and small trees to pull themselves up. While the men appreciated the cover the smoke provided, they had difficulty getting a breath through their gas masks. With impaired breathing and serious fatigue, they needed to stop and rest from time to time. The bluff rose about 125 feet at that spot, but Milo thought it must have been at least 100 yards, as it took him three hours to make the climb. A few men were injured by German mines, but most made it safely to the top. Once there, the GIs tore off their gas masks and most threw them away.[2] They grabbed a few moments to sit down and take a deep breath, away from the fierce fighting, thick smoke, and hard climbing.

Milo was struck by the enormity of what he'd just gone through. He realized that thinking about his father was the only thing that had kept him going. He knew he was part of a momentous occasion and worried about what his father would think about how he acted. His dad had been a soldier in World War I, a sergeant in the artillery, and would understand what combat was like. With the insanity of war all around him, Milo's main concern was that his father might criticize him for not handling things perfectly.

Chapter 7

Killing Fields

It was about 1:00 p.m. by then, a cloudy day, but at least the rain had stopped. After a short rest period, Milo ordered his group of men up and headed them out toward the west. Within minutes they met another group of soldiers who had made it up the bluff. These men were led by an officer, a Captain Johnson, who Milo recalled being from Green Bay, Wisconsin. He was a company commander in the 16th Regiment, 1st Division, and had quite a few of his troops with him. Milo thought he was an old guy, at least 28 or 29. The captain asked him, "How many of your men got to the top?" Milo said he didn't know.

"Take your men, count 'em, redistribute ammo, and wait for me." Milo gave the officer a "Yessir," and went back to his men. His men, the captain had said. He was being treated like an officer, leading a force as big as a company. It was pretty heady stuff for a nineteen-year-old buck private on his first day of combat.

Once Milo had his crew organized, the captain directed them inland toward Vierville. "Flaten," he said, "take your men and go in that field and we'll go into the next one." Milo and his group climbed over a hedgerow and entered an enclosed farm field. This was the bocage, a French word meaning a grove or small forest. The word is used in English, too, and describes a mixture of woodland and pasture with hedgerows and sunken roads.

Agriculture abounds in Normandy. Apple trees grow in profusion in its rich soil, and dairy farming has been carried on there for centuries. The GIs had been told there were hedgerows in France and knew what they were. They were common in England: grassy earthen berms, or embankments, two or three feet high, with trees and prickly shrubs growing on top. Farmers used them as fences to mark the boundaries of pastures and keep their cattle confined. Given all the intelligence gathered and preparations made for this invasion, Milo found it astounding no one had noticed French hedgerows differed greatly from the English variety. They were thicker, taller, and contained more dense vegetation. In fact, Normandy's were bigger and more compacted than any in the rest of France.

The pastures these hedgerows defined had existed hundreds of years before D-Day, many since Roman times. As the shrubs on top of the hills had grown, their roots dug deeper into the soil and intertwined, raising the embankment higher. The briars or other thorny plants growing across the top were like barbed wire, and their interlocked roots made the mounds almost impenetrable. Norman hedgerows averaged four to eight feet high, but some topped fifteen feet. Narrow access lanes surrounded groups of pastures; farmers used them to take their cows into the fields in the morning, and back to the barn at night. Each pasture had a gate at one end opening off the lane for access. With the passage of hundreds of years, the lanes had sunk lower and lower. By 1944 many were deeply depressed, and those with overarching trees were comparable to tunnels.

GIs tried entering the fields at their gates, but the Germans were well prepared for them. They had been in the area for months, setting their gun emplacements and sighting them in. Every gate had at least one machine gun trained on it, and trying to enter a field that way was suicidal. Norman hedgerows were ideal for the Germans' defense of the area and a real headache for the Allies. In the days to come, many GIs likely thought "bocage" was a direct translation of the word "hell."

As Milo's group began its passage into the pastures, he continued to act as 1st scout, the first soldier to enter each field. In the first pasture he entered he heard shooting on either side of him, but met no resistance. In the next field, he and his men met occasional rifle fire and artillery, but there were no direct hits. As the GIs continued forward, they came to the brow of a hill and saw a large, odd-looking bush in the distance. Captain Johnson and Milo met and talked about whether they should take a look at it. The captain suggested they ought to ignore it and continue going inland as far as they could. Milo was awed an officer would consider his opinion valuable and naturally agreed with the older man's conclusion.

They continued pressing forward until they heard a lot of commotion and shooting. The fuss seemed to be located about a quarter of a mile behind them, in the area of the odd bush they'd seen. The captain called for a few of his men to check out what was happening and told Milo to meet him about 25 yards from the bush. Milo's unit snuck back on one of the sunken roads and crossed a hedgerow. When they got to the "bush" they found a large open field without any hedgerows, covering the entire top of the hill. In the middle of it was a huge concrete gun emplacement. A camouflage net with bushes scattered on top covered it all. From their present vantage point, it was quite conspicuous, as the cover was a different color of green than its surroundings.

The weapon itself was immense, bolted to a concrete pad ten feet deep with nuts as big as a man's fist. To Milo the gun looked as massive as a battleship's armament, fifteen to twenty feet long, and seemingly over ten inches in caliber. Next to the gun was a concrete building with a steel door, likely the crew's quarters, he thought. The cannon was aimed directly at Omaha Beach, obviously intended for use against incoming ships and invading troops.

The captain's patrol couldn't figure out what the yelling and hollering was all about. Milo saw some GIs coming up the hill, but couldn't see what they were shooting at. Then the door in the concrete structure opened and someone thrust out a stick with a white cloth tied to it. Six men in greenish-gray uniforms carrying pieces of white cloth walked out of the building and surrendered to

Milo. He'd never taken prisoners before and didn't know what to do. One of his men got some tent ropes, and they tied the Germans' hands together.

The bothersome sailor, the forward observer from the beach, was still hanging around, pestering Milo with questions. No matter how much Milo tried to put the man off, he kept asking. Seeing a way to kill two birds with one stone, Milo gave the sailor a rifle and told him to take the prisoners down the hill to the POW area at Regimental Headquarters. Milo was pretty sure Regimental HQ was still out at sea on a ship, but he wasn't so much concerned about what happened to the Germans. He was more interested in getting the pesky sailor out of his hair.

Once rid of the captives, Captain Johnson, Milo, and a soldier from Arkansas nicknamed Arkie climbed into the pit where the gun sat. German infantry had begun attacking them, and the three men knew they had little time. Captain Johnson produced a thermite grenade he was carrying. These grenades became so intensely hot when ignited the heat could kill anyone within a ten-foot radius. Milo was acutely aware of the danger. Back on the beach, a German bullet had struck and ignited a thermite grenade hanging from a GI's uniform. Milo and the other soldiers in the area had to watch the man burn to death and listen to him scream. There was no way to save him.

The cannon barrel pointed up at an angle and the muzzle was too high for Milo to reach. They found some German ammunition boxes, and the captain said, "I'll stack the boxes, you climb up." By standing on the crates, Milo could just reach the end of the barrel, but his perch was quite wobbly. He worried he might fall after activating the grenade and not be able to get away from it. Standing up on tiptoe on the boxes, he pulled the pin, let the handle go, and placed the grenade in the barrel. It didn't move. Milo guessed it might have caught on the barrel's rifling, and with just a couple of seconds before it would ignite, he jumped up and shoved his hand into the barrel to knock it loose. He could hear it then, tumbling down into the cannon. A few seconds later smoke came out of the barrel, and the receiver turned red hot and then white. The men could tell the grenade had melted enough metal to render the gun useless. Captain Johnson got out a notebook and asked Milo his name and what outfit he was with. Milo wouldn't know until months later the officer had put him up for an award for his bravery.

With the annoying sailor and his prisoners gone and the gun out of commission, it was time to go back to the original plan. The three men climbed out of the gun emplacement and proceeded on their original course. Soon they ran into a lieutenant from Captain Johnson's company with some of his men, and they all went back to the area they'd reached before the gun incident. By now it was late afternoon and the captain told Milo to spread his men out along the hedgerow and await further orders. As they stood by, twelve members of Milo's E Company found their way to his group and joined it. They had also scaled the bluff under the cover of smoke. The accumulated assortment of soldiers dug in and stayed there overnight.

At first light the next morning, the Germans began firing artillery and mortars at them and later attacked. Milo spent his second day in France in vicious, nearly continuous firefights, until night fell.

The next day, a soldier came running up to the hedgerow where Milo's group was located. He called together all the men from Milo's 2nd Battalion and told them, "You guys are supposed to go back to that sunken road and someone will take you back to your unit."

Milo realized his days as a de facto officer and a leader of men were over, and he was dejected. He'd been commanding his own unit since hitting the beach, and now he was being sent back to be a lowly buck private again. The troops fell back to the road where a lieutenant from the 2nd Battalion was in charge. Milo checked out the assembled group and, of the forty or fifty men gathered there, not one was from his platoon. The lieutenant ordered the men to double-time down the lane, and as he ran, Milo recognized a few people, mainly battalion officers. Then someone said, "If you're from E Company, your unit's up here. Go up this road to the hedgerows and you'll run into them."

When Milo arrived at his company's location, one of the first people he met was Captain Steward, the CO.[1] The captain greeted Milo in the same annoyed manner he usually did: "Flaten, where the hell have you been?" Milo told him what had happened. Hardly any men from the old company were there, perhaps fifteen or so out of the original 180. Milo saw only one man from his boat group, As far as he knew, the rest had all died.[2] That didn't surprise him. He was pretty sure anyone who didn't get shot coming off the boat's ramp would have drowned. Even with their life jackets, the staggering weight of all the gear they carried would have pulled them under. He knew none of the others except Hirsch could swim well and was sure none had the intensive Boy Scout and Sea Scout lifesaving training that had kept him alive.[3]

While Milo had been busy commanding his own group, E Company had received about a hundred replacements. Those men and the remaining original troops had been combined and reorganized into squads and platoons, but even with the replacements, every unit was still under strength. Regardless, that night the reconstituted company made their way to Vierville-sur-Mer (Vierville on the Sea; many communities along the coast had the "sur-Mer" designation added to their name). Vierville was a little town a half-mile inland and a mile and a half west of where Milo had come ashore, and had been liberated earlier that afternoon by GIs who landed nearby. Calling it a town is perhaps overly generous. Farms and settlements in Normandy were not like those in the US; farmhouses were not separated by many acres of land. In Normandy, three or four or possibly more farmhouses were built close together, like the hub of a wheel, and the various owners' fields radiated outward from them like spokes. That small cluster of homes, plus a church and perhaps a wine shop, was considered a town. The farmers shared outbuildings. Livestock often lived on the ground floor of their houses, while the families lived above. Vierville was such a place.

Milo and a cohort dug a foxhole where they spent the night, as they would for many nights to come. Only one man slept at a time, while the other stood guard, peering over the edge of the hole toward the next hedgerow, watching for the enemy. Each stood a four-hour watch, so neither man ever got a full night's sleep. They didn't have packs or sleeping bags, but slept on their raincoats. For warmth, they used the other guy's raincoat and/or shelter-half over them. Each man carried a canvas shelter-half. Two halves could be joined together to make a two-man tent, but they rarely set one up because foxholes were much safer.

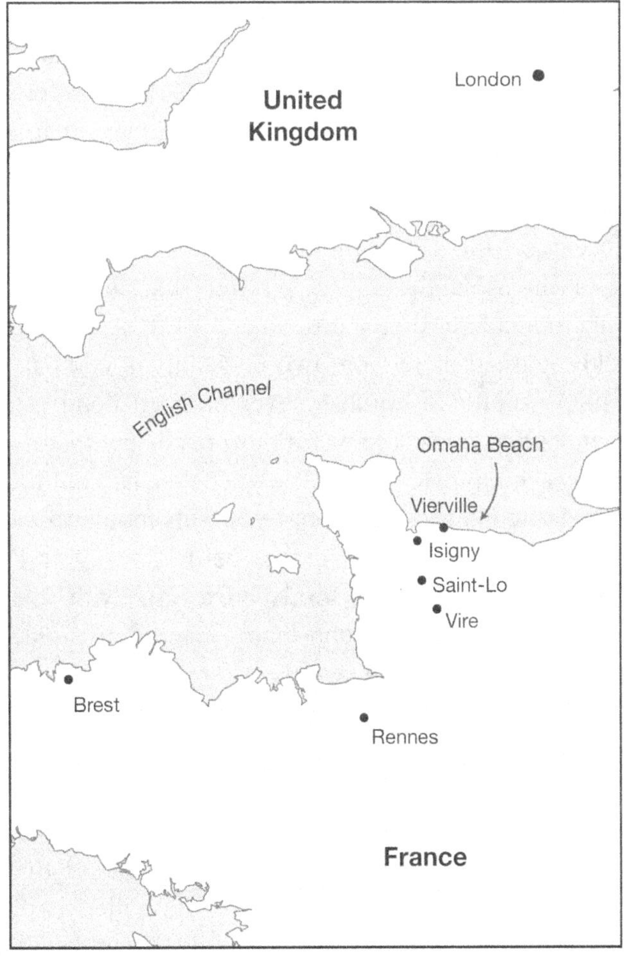

Milo's locations D-Day through September 24, 1944

Sometimes both men slept at the same time. The order would be "every other hole," which meant while they were sleeping, both the guys in the next foxhole were keeping watch. Even though it was the end of June, nights were uncomfortably cold, and they slept curled up like Z's, just as a man might spoon with his wife. They thought nothing of it; it was merely a way to keep warm. But their rest lasted only half a night, as they'd then be awakened to stand watch while the two men in the other hole slept. Sometimes, when they weren't expecting an attack, they'd forgo the foxhole and sleep on the ground. Digging foxholes in Normandy was nothing like it had been in boot camp, in the sandy soils of Florida. The ground in this region was compact and hard, full of rocks and stones. It took a great deal of effort to dig a hole deep enough for safety and big enough for two men to lie down. They considered it a gift when they could get by for a night without having to exert that much effort.

This became Milo's way of life for the coming months. Days were full of intense fighting and physical exertion, while nights were passed in a hole or on the ground and were never long enough. Milo quickly learned there were two constants in combat: fear and exhaustion. A soldier in combat never stopped being scared and never got enough sleep. There was a third persistent factor for Milo: he was always thirsty. He ate apples whenever he could to quench his thirst, and often kept a pebble or two in his mouth to keep saliva coming. He had never been a smoker before, but after D-Day he started smoking the cigarettes furnished to GIs with their rations and got hooked. He smoked constantly, except at night, when it wasn't safe. After a while, he switched to cigars and chain-smoked them from then on. All the while he was in combat, he was terrified. One way he handled his fear was to smoke and chomp on his cigars.[4]

The next day, E Company set out for Isigny-sur-Mer, about ten miles to the southwest. Milo pronounced the name of the town as "Eye-seen'-ee," and said that's what the GIs called it during the war. French speakers pronounced it "Eez'-nie." [5] Unlike Vierville, it was a fair-sized town with large square in its center that contained a monument and a fountain. When Milo's unit arrived, most German forces had been driven out, but there was still scattered shooting in the area. Milo and the other men were sent out to clear the town of any remaining enemy. That meant going house-to-house, searching inside and outside each building. It was terrible, dangerous work. Any Germans-in-hiding shot GIs as soon as they appeared. Not only was there considerable risk involved, but the task was endlessly repetitious. It was drudgery required of riflemen in each town and city they liberated: nasty, perilous duty that frightened and traumatized them.

It took a few days of fighting, but eventually the sound of gunfire had almost stopped, though some was still occasionally coming from large German guns, tank-mounted "88s." These cannons, 88 millimeters in caliber, were originally designed to be anti-aircraft weapons. They proved to be so efficient the Germans converted them into artillery pieces. Later, they mounted the guns on tanks and other self-propelled armored vehicles. One of their tactics utilized a bombed or blown-out house in which the first floor was gone. They'd drive a tank or armored vehicle into the basement and poke the 88's barrel out a window, providing them with both partial cover and a broad range of fire. Milo saw more than one of those weapons positioned in basements in Isigny.

On June 14th, after the town was cleared, the GIs returned to the town square. Milo watched as an elderly gentleman wearing a high stovepipe hat stepped out of one of the buildings. Other people followed, some carrying flowers and champagne. Milo got word the man in the tall hat was a very important person, the mayor of Isigny. A party of Frenchmen, some dressed in military uniforms, joined the citizens. Milo gathered they were members of the Free French Forces, the independent resistance organization which had been fighting Germans since long before D-Day.[6] After a few minutes there was a flurry of activity from the crowd, and the leader of the Free French Forces, Charles de Gaulle, appeared.[7]

He was a very tall man, around 6'6", and wore a French military uniform. He was there to give a talk, and after he arrived more townspeople gathered. Paramount News was on hand to film the scene. As Milo watched the little ceremony, he kept worrying about the still present 88s that had been shooting just a while earlier, but fortunately, they were silent. After the speech the crowd left, and the GIs were ordered to move out. They resumed their attack, moving ahead toward the retreating Germans. Finally, close to midnight, they were told to take a break and Milo's company was relieved. He was exhausted. As soon as he was about 25 feet behind the lines, he flopped to the ground and was asleep within minutes.

Chapter 8

War-Torn

The following morning, Milo and his companions started out for their next objective, the city of Saint-Lô (often abbreviated St Lô), about fourteen miles south of Isigny. Invasion planners had optimistically predicted GIs would take Saint-Lô on D-Day itself, but that didn't happen for several reasons. The Americans were stymied by heavy German resistance. The intensity of battle and the accuracy and density of the enemy's artillery increased with each day. While there were not always bullets flying around from firefights, there was always the sound of artillery shells sailing overhead and striking nearby. Also, this was the rainiest summer Normandy had experienced in many years. The ground turned to mud, making it miserable for the men and nearly impassable for vehicles. And, as noted, nobody had prepared the troops to fight in the French bocage. One day they might get ahead a quarter of a mile, and another advance only two hedgerows. And each day they would typically lose nearly a hundred men to casualties.

GIs approached every hedgerow cautiously, entering the field it enclosed with great care. Sometimes there were Germans waiting for them, in which case they would back off in a hurry. If no enemy was encountered, 1st scout Milo would go over the row and begin across the field, his rifle at the ready. The 2nd scout would go over the hedgerow and wait there until Milo reached the next row. If there were no Germans, Milo signaled the 2nd scout, who alerted the rest of the men. They would come over the hedgerow and all would advance to Milo's position. They repeated this process over and over, hedgerow after hedgerow.

Between the beach and Saint-Lô, E Company had several fire-fights in which Milo experienced a unique form of warfare, something he'd not been trained for or ever heard about. The Germans would shoot everything they had in rifle firepower at the Americans. The GIs would assume the Germans were trying to force them to keep their heads down so they could attack. But instead of hiding from the lead thrown their way, the Americans fired back as fast and as hard as they could. If they were in foxholes, one of the two men would stand up and fire all eight rounds in his rifle and then duck down to load another clip. His hole-mate would jump up and fire eight rounds as quickly as he could, and they would repeat the process as long as they could. If they were not in foxholes, they found cover and did essentially the same thing. It was a hectic and lethal exchange of bullets. Each GI carried six or seven bandoliers, each with ten clips of eight bullets in it, close to 500 rounds per man. Large crates of ammo were constantly trucked up to the front lines to re-supply them. The men used all the ammo they could get, and sometimes couldn't get enough to sustain their attack.

One evening Milo's battalion got into a particularly ferocious and long-lasting firefight. Word came down they were surrounded, and other GI units couldn't get through to bring them rations, water, or ammunition. There were plenty of apples around, and nobody was starving, but they were running short of ammo. Another company brought a .30 caliber machine gun up to the top of a short hedgerow where Milo was located and started firing, making some progress. Milo and his men couldn't see the Germans and the Germans couldn't see them, but the American machine gun was close enough to the gate to be visible to the enemy. Suddenly, with a loud explosion, the machine gunner and his assistant were both hit and killed by mortar fire.

Milo, by now a sergeant, reacted quickly. He climbed down the hedgerow towards the German position and pulled the ammunition belt out of the machine gun. Germans fired at him, but by lying low on the ground he avoided being hit. He yelled to his men to give him all the empty rifle clips lying around, and began removing cartridges from the belt and inserting them in clips. He could only use two out of three shells, as every third bullet was a tracer and would ruin a rifle. When the clips were full, one of his men passed them out to other troops. When the first belt was empty, he repeated the process with the belts in two other boxes of ammo. Despite being under constant fire, he stayed hunched down at his task until every usable bullet had been reloaded. His bravery and leadership were duly noted, and he was decorated for his actions.

As combat progressed, Milo realized the Germans were doing something odd. It didn't occur with each fight, but it happened often enough he took notice. On these occasions, he would climb over a hedgerow, run two-thirds of the way across the field with no resistance, and wave the 2nd scout forward. The Germans would immediately shoot the 2nd scout just as he climbed off the hedgerow. Milo didn't understand why he, the 1st scout, wasn't the one shot upon entering the field. He thought maybe they let the 1st scout go so they could trap the whole unit and take more casualties. But that didn't account for them shooting the 2nd Scout while the rest of the men were still hidden. Whether his reasoning made sense or not, Milo kept the job of 1st scout because he felt he had a better chance of not getting shot.

Not that he wasn't getting injured. He got hit quite a few times, but most of his wounds were minor. It was usually something like a piece of shrapnel grazing him, or a stone chip thrown up by an exploding shell. He'd go to the aid station, get a bandage, or stitches, or whatever treatment was needed, and be back in combat within an hour or two. The clerk there was supposed to alert a soldier's family any time he was wounded. The first few times Milo got treated his parents received a telegram from the War Department which said, in effect, "Your son has been lightly wounded but has returned to duty." Milo assumed the wires were driving his parents crazy, and after three or four had been sent, he told the clerk not to send any more.

But besides minor wounds, he also incurred more serious injuries while on the way to Saint-Lô. On one occasion his unit was following a road forward. Some men were on the road itself while Milo and others were advancing through woods bordering the roadway. The group on the road came upon an empty German tank that was out of commission and blocking the roadway. When they checked it out, they found the German tank crew had booby-trapped it, placing twelve landmines around the vehicle before they ran off. Engineers removed the mines and stacked them together in the ditch on one side of the road. An MP was stationed there to direct traffic into the ditch on the other side of the road. After a while, for some reason the MP left the area. An American Army truck came up and drove around the tank in the "wrong" ditch, the one with the mines. All twelve exploded together, destroying the truck and its occupants, and injuring many GIs in the area. Milo was near enough to the blast it blew out one of his eardrums. Fortunately, he wasn't hit by any shrapnel.

Another injury occurred, which involved the German's new practice of shooting 2nd scouts, as noted above. Milo's company was still slogging to Saint-Lô cross-country through the hedgerows. When they came to the next row, just as he had been doing, Milo cut a hole in the brush with his bayonet and climbed over the embankment. He was about two thirds across the field and things still seemed quiet, so he signaled the 2nd scout, a soldier named Nelson, to come forward. Nelson came through the same hole Milo had cut, and the Germans shot him as soon as he was off the row. They had gun emplacements hidden all around the field in the shrubbery and opened fire with several machine guns. Nelson lay on the ground yelling he'd been hit, and Milo found himself standing out in the open, a hundred feet or more from the rest of his unit. In fact, he was closer to the German-occupied hedgerow than his own troops.

Milo's battalion commander had been complaining mortars weren't being used enough, and had sent H Company, the weapons company, along with E Company on this mission. A forward observer for H Company saw what was happening and called in mortar fire on the Germans. Shells began exploding on and behind the hedgerow where the Germans were located. Some, though, fell short and landed quite close to Milo. He was stunned and looked for a hiding place. He spotted an empty German foxhole close to the hedgerow, ran to it, and jumped in. As he lay in the hole listening to shells exploding around him, he thought, "What the hell am I going to do now?" He was close enough to hear Germans talking on the other side of the embankment and about a hundred and fifty feet away from his own lines and safety. Nelson was still lying where he fell. Two GI medics came out on the field to get him and the Germans fired at them. The Geneva Conventions prohibited shooting at medics displaying Red Cross symbols. Milo figured the armbands those guys were wearing were so dirty the Red Cross emblem couldn't be seen. The medics ran back over the hedgerow, leaving Nelson still yelling. After what seemed to Milo a long time, the medics came back carrying a white flag with a large red cross. Milo heard the Germans saying, "Nicht schießen" (don't shoot).

He assessed his situation and concluded there wasn't much he could do. It was too far for him to make it safely back to his unit. He didn't think his guys would come out to get him, but at least they'd keep an eye on him as long as there was daylight. He'd have to wait for dark to get back. Just in case there was a chance he could make a run for it now, however, he checked things out. Peeking over the lip of the foxhole, he saw no Germans. He climbed out of the hole and tiptoed into the shrubbery on the hedgerow. He could hear German voices clearly and guessed they were about fifteen yards away. While climbing up the row, the camouflage netting on his helmet caught on a small branch. He shook it free, got near the crest of the embankment and slowly raised his head to look over. The face of an enemy soldier was only two or three inches from his own. The German was clearly just as surprised as he was. Milo ran back and dropped into the foxhole, and the Germans started hollering at him. He presumed they were telling him to surrender, but was too scared to do anything. Then German hand grenades (called potato mashers because of their appearance) started coming over the hedgerow. Most landed harmlessly out in the field, quite a distance from his location. At the time, Milo was surprised the Germans had such poor aim. Thinking about it later, he decided they were probably very skittish about throwing their grenades. Much of German weaponry was manufactured by non-Germans in slave labor camps. Many of those workers hated Nazis, and were doing everything they could to sabotage German arms and ammunition. German grenades were particularly untrustworthy and had a reputation for exploding before they could be thrown. Milo thought that might account for the krauts not taking the time to aim more precisely.

By late afternoon, the Germans finally quit throwing grenades at him, and he felt a little hope. But just after they stopped, H Company began firing its mortars again. Milo groaned and thought he'd never get out of there now. At that moment, something landed in his foxhole and exploded, blowing him clear out of the hole onto the parapet, the loose soil around the foxhole's edge. It could have been a German grenade or an American mortar; he would never know. Before the explosion, he hadn't had the nerve to leave his hole and run back. But he was out of it now, and figured he might as well make the most of it. He reached back into the foxhole for his rifle and found it had been blown to pieces. It had been leaning up against the side of the hole, and whatever exploded had hit the receiver of the weapon. The rifle must have absorbed most of the shrapnel because Milo was hit by only one piece, a small metal fragment which buried itself on the back of his little finger. He realized with some surprise his M1 had saved his life. He also realized, however, that he was bleeding from every opening in his body: his eyes, his nose, his ears, and every other orifice. That concerned him a great deal, so he got up and ran toward his own unit as fast as he could.

One of his cohorts saw him coming, opened the gate for him, and he ran right through. He was so out of breath he just hit the ground and the other guy dragged him back farther to safety. He was panting heavily, and his uniform was covered with blood. When he looked up, there was Captain Steward standing over him. "Flaten," he said. "Where the hell have you been?" Milo told him what had happened. "Oh," the CO said, "I heard there was a guy out there. You don't look so good; you better get down to the aid station."

Milo walked back two hedgerows where a jeep with stretchers waited. He climbed on a stretcher and was driven back to battalion aid station. A doctor there examined him and said he had suffered a concussion and then a type of seizure, which caused many of his blood vessels to rupture. One of his lungs had collapsed. The piece of metal that hit his little finger had severed a tendon, so the doctor reattached the severed ends and put a bandage on it. The surgery was excellent; the hand would never be a problem after that. However, his other, healthy eardrum had ruptured from the force of the explosion and his hearing would never again be normal.

Corpsmen put him on a stretcher atop another jeep, this one carrying four other guys on stretchers, and drove him to the Regimental Aid Station. Another doctor looked at him and sent him to the 13th Evacuation Hospital located about ten miles behind the line. Medics carried him off the jeep and laid his stretcher down on the ground. Several nubs, stubby little legs on the stretcher, held it a few inches above the dirt. He lay there quite a while among other wounded soldiers. Although he was fading in and out of consciousness, he wasn't feeling any pain. The man next to him was a sergeant from E company named Damon who'd been hit the day before. He was a fellow midwesterner from Minnesota, and Milo loved being able to speak with people whose language sounded like his. The two talked at length about the war and what had happened to them. Milo noticed everyone called the man Sergeant Damon. Milo was a sergeant too and felt he was entitled to the same respect, but everyone just called him Flaten. The next morning Sgt. Damon wasn't there, and Milo asked a corpsman where he was. The medic said he had died during the night. Milo felt a considerable loss. Damon was one of very few GIs he ever got to know well.

Milo remained at the hospital for about ten days. It was a unique experience for him. GIs there were without helmets, and female nurses cared for him (this was the closest to the front that women were allowed). Eventually he felt better and soon was walking around. Neither he nor the doctors thought there was much wrong with him. As usual, not enough replacements were being sent to the front, so wounded men were rushed back to their outfits as quickly as possible. A doctor told Milo he was going to test him to make sure his breathing was back to normal. He had Milo run full speed down to the end of the field, climb over the hedgerow, climb back over it and run back to the starting point. The doctor then had him spit in a coffee can. There was no blood in his saliva, so the doc said he was ready to return to duty. They discharged him from the hospital and took him back to his company. It's quite likely one thing was the same, that Captain Steward asked where the hell he'd been, but everything else was different. The company was in a different location, and was down to about fifty men. After being gone only ten days, Milo recognized only a few.

Besides changes in location and personnel, there was also a tactical change afoot. After all the firefights they'd had, it was clear fire and maneuver wasn't working. The Americans changed their mode of operation to "fire superiority," which meant everybody would shoot at the enemy continuously, without letup. If Milo spotted Germans, he would give the signal, and the entire unit would cross the hedgerow together and form a skirmish line. Everyone would shoot as much and as often as they could, and run at the Germans while hollering and yelling like madmen. Milo likened it to Indians chasing cowboys in the movies. The maneuver apparently scared Germans, as they usually made fast retreats and were gone when the GIs arrived. Milo considered it the infantry's most effective tactic and wished it had been taught in England. Notably, however, it didn't work if the Germans they encountered were Nazi SS,[1] considered the toughest of all German soldiers. All the combat training films Milo had seen in boot camp showed the enemy as being Japanese, a race of people generally smaller than Americans. Many of the SS men were as big as or bigger than Milo, and they all fought savagely, often hand to hand and with rifle butts, knives, and bayonets. They were hard, dangerous men, thoroughly committed to Nazi ideology, and had taken solemn oaths to fight to the death. They didn't run away from anything.

The fighting Milo's division faced those days shortly after D-Day was all uphill, with Germans seeming to have every advantage. Pre-invasion plans had assumed GIs would advance to Caen (more than forty miles west of Saint-Lô) by the second or third day after hitting the beach. In large part because nobody had identified the actual features of the French landscape, the troops were weeks behind schedule, and thousands of GIs had been killed and wounded.[2] The infantry needed help, and it would have been a great to have tanks enter the fields first to clear the way for infantrymen to advance. Though tanks were available, they were ineffective in the bocage. They couldn't push their way through the embankments because of the intertwined vegetation and roots. When they tried going over the top, they exposed their lightly armored underbellies and the Germans easily knocked them out.

American soldiers were known for their ingenuity and ability to improvise, and many engineers and mechanics had been looking for solutions to the hedgerow problem ever since D-Day. Several divisions, including the 29th, had assigned people to the task. One method the 29th tried involved using explosives to blow a hole in the dirt big enough for a tank to pass through. But they found it took too much dynamite to do this, more than would be available. They discovered that steel poles welded on the front of a tank could ram holes deep into the mound, and smaller amounts of explosives placed in them were more effective. But in the end, men in several divisions simultaneously came up with essentially the same solution: steel tines welded on the front of the tanks. They were made from parts of the German hedgehog tank defenses on the beach and mounted a couple feet above the ground, much like those on a forklift truck. So equipped, a tank charging forward at the right speed dug its tines into the embankments with sufficient force to make a hole it could get through. GIs called them Rhinos because of their appearance. Had the Allies known the size and density of French hedgerows, chances are Rhinos, or something similarly effective, would have been developed before D-Day. One can only speculate how many lives might have been saved.

Chapter 9

Ready, Set, Stop

The day after Milo returned from the hospital, the 29th advanced into the valley where Saint-Lô, their objective, was located. The entire division had been engaged in almost continuous hard fighting leading up to this point, and its commanders worried the men were too exhausted to be effective in an attack on the town. While Saint-Lô itself had limited military value, it was the gateway to Vire, a city of much greater importance. The XIX Corps Commander, Gen. Gerhardt's boss, was strongly pressuring the 29th Division to take Saint-Lô posthaste. Gerhard managed to amp up that pressure to a degree where it seemed he was asking physical impossibilities of his troops. His orders to his regimental commanders were blistering, but it was the GIs who suffered the consequences of his commands, daily, hourly, and minute-by-minute. They were the ones who felt the stress, fear, and exhaustion from the constant combat. They didn't know the general had promised his regimental commanders a whole week off for the division if it captured Saint-Lô immediately. Although a few units had a day or two of rest to prepare for the assault, most of the 29th didn't, and kept trudging ahead towards the target.

Milo's 116th Regiment was advancing along the left side of an elevated area called the Martinville Ridge, named after the Village of Martinville located on the outskirts of Saint-Lô.[1] The 115th was on the other side of the ridge, and the 175th was in reserve. By July 12th they were about three miles east of the city, but as they continued moving west on the 13th and 14th, German shelling increased to an unprecedented level. The Germans had 13 artillery battalions lined up in the surrounding hills, cannons hub-to-hub, and were pounding away at American positions. Explosions were so intense and constant they blew all the vegetation off the tops of the hedgerows. The GIs were forced to stop where they were and wait for the bombardment to subside. They dug their foxholes as close to the base of the hedgerows as possible to get the most cover available. The embankment formed a wall in front of them, shielding them from shells which hit ahead of it. Some rounds, though, were landing on their side of the rows, so they kept digging their foxholes deeper and farther into the bank as time went on. The constant blasts made the earth shake, and the vibrations caused anything a soldier set on the parapet beside his foxhole to fall into the hole. Branches and foliage the troops used to cover their holes fell in too. They couldn't hear anything except the roar of the blasts, and all they could see were the four hedgerow walls of the pasture. Milo thought it fitting American soldiers were often called dogfaces, as they were living like animals. After days of huddling in the dirt, they were covered with grime. Their faces were so full of mud one could only see their teeth and the whites of their eyes. They hadn't had fresh food or vegetables for almost two weeks and were subsisting only on apples and their remaining rations. Some of the young men's hair turned white. No one knew if that was caused by a nutritional deficiency or sheer terror, but for Milo the ordeal was forty times worse than Omaha Beach. He was certain he would die there.

The barrage eventually stopped, and the men could climb out of their holes. Pastures in the area had been full of cattle before the bombardment. Now in the field Milo occupied lay the bloated corpses of nearly fifty cows, along with the bodies of many dead soldiers, some GIs, but mostly Germans. American Graves Registration soldiers removed killed GIs from the battlefield as soon as possible, but Germans were a lot slower at it. The resulting stench and the smoke and smells from tons of explosives were ghastly and overpowering.

A lone German soldier carrying a white flag and wearing a white tunic bearing a medic's red cross suddenly appeared. He asked if the Americans would consent to a truce long enough for each side to remove the dead bodies. The CO agreed, and for two hours, no weapons were fired while men from each army removed all the corpses. Some GIs suspected the German who approached them wasn't a medic but an infantryman. They thought he was using the occasion to spy on American positions and manpower. Perhaps so, but at least the corpses had been retrieved. And as soon as the bodies were gone, the shooting and killing started again.

Gen. Gerhard visited the front on the 14th and noted the rotting cattle carcasses still there, creating a noxious odor. Being a fastidious man, he ordered all the animals buried forthwith. During his stay there was no way he could fail to notice his men were not wearing their helmet chinstraps, or that officers' insignia were missing. Or that white stripes on the back of officers' and NCOs' helmets had been rubbed with dirt and were almost invisible. No one saluted, and the men didn't address each other by rank. (GIs knew the Germans would shoot officers and NCO's first, if they could tell who they were.) All that might have upset the old martinet, but victory was plainly more important to him. He knew better than to say anything about it.

Captain Steward ordered Milo to pick out a few men for a mission. "You're going into Saint-Lô tonight," he said. Milo was to lead a patrol flank-guarding a tank and some division officers, including Brigadier General Norman Cota, Assistant Commander of the 29th Division. Milo picked four men for the patrol, and the tank and soldiers entered St. Lo with no resistance. The town was largely unscathed. While there was rubble here and there, most of the structures were not damaged. The enlisted men camped outside in tents while the officers stayed in a vacant house. Milo had to enter the home several times and saw that none of the contents had been harmed or destroyed. Pictures still hung on the walls, and everything was intact. While he was not privy to the group's mission, it wasn't hard to gather that the officers were figuring out how best to capture the city. After two days, the entourage returned to the Martinville area. Milo and his men rejoined their company, while the tank and officers continued back to division HQ.

On July 15th, the division renewed its attack, with US artillery heavily shelling German positions. That allowed the 116th's 1st and 2nd Battalions to move forward faster than they had before. The regimental CO called off fighting as night approached, but the 2nd Battalion, which was in the lead, didn't get the order. It kept advancing to the town of La Madeleine, half a mile ahead of the others. That left a substantial gap between the 2nd and 1st Battalions which Germans quickly occupied. They cut the Americans' phone wires and blocked supplies from reaching Milo's battalion. Division commanders were more than concerned.

The following morning, the 115th attacked the occupying Germans, but couldn't advance more than 300 yards. By this time, Milo and his colleagues were hungry, thirsty, and without provisions. Fortunately, that night one of the men located an abandoned farm well which provided them with water. Finally, on the 17th, the 116th's 3rd Battalion made it through and brought supplies.

Each morning platoon leaders briefed their men on what the general attack would be for the day. That day, the 17th, the officers told their charges Saint-Lô was about to be bombed, and then they would enter the city to take it. Soon the men heard a muffled hum that continually grew louder. It was the sound of airplane engines, hundreds of them. The morning had dawned bright and sunny, and GIs looked skyward to watch the spectacle. While the bombers themselves were too high to be seen, they were definitely heard. The earth shook and trembled from the roar. When the noise appeared to be directly overhead, the soldiers saw what looked like rain falling from the sky. It was the sun flashing on bombs being dropped on Saint-Lô. At times they saw larger blips, like stars twinkling, from sunlight reflecting off the fuselages of the planes.

The next day, July 18th, the 116th Regiment advanced further along the ridge and took up a position on the main road leading into Saint-Lô. The 115th was nearby on a parallel road, also ready to enter the city. Gen. Gerhardt was about to give the two regiments the order to attack when he realized resistance would be strongest against those units' positions, and at the last minute changed the battle plan. He had Gen. Cota put together a task force of tanks and men and go into the town in a different, lightly fortified section. The ploy was successful, the battle short, and the task force took control of the city that day. Milo's 116th Regiment had no part in the battle, but sat it out in reserve about 100 yards from the city's edge.

After the task force cleared the area, the rest of the division was trucked through the city, following the advancing American troops. Milo sat on the tailgate and had an open view of his surroundings. The amount of damage he saw astounded him. Almost the entire city had been leveled, first by bombing, and then by artillery fire. Hardly anything was left but rubble. He had difficulty believing it was the same city he had recently visited. He also passed by the soon-to-be famous flag-draped casket set up near the Church of Notre Dame in the city's main square. Artillery fire had killed Major Thomas Howie, CO of the 116th's 3rd Battalion. Gen. Gerhardt had ordered his coffin displayed at the church, and newsreel cameras and correspondents were paying a great deal of attention to it. Folks back in the US saw it in newsreels, but because of censorship, the Army didn't give the fallen officer's name. He became known in the States as the Major of Saint-Lô. Even though the officer had been something of a hero, Milo still thought the display was showboating, and didn't approve.

Gen. Gerhardt made good on his promise, and gave the 29th the next seven days in reserve. It was their first time out of combat in nearly a month and a half. On July 19th, the 116th moved by shuttle march into an assembly area about five miles north of Saint-Lô. Perhaps the most satisfying thing they experienced was the reduction of fear they felt resulting from the lack of lead flying around them.

Likely the next most satisfying was taking a shower and

changing into clean, new uniforms. The shower was anything but fancy, and took place on the flatbed trailer of a semi-trailer truck. The men lined up, and when their turn came, climbed onto the trailer, several at a time. They stood under showerheads that were turned off. At the blow of a whistle an attendant turned the water on for one minute. The men then soaped themselves and gave a signal when they were ready. At another whistle blast, the water came on for three minutes, allowing them to scrub and rinse off the soap. Luxurious or not, it was a godsend. The men also slept in tents, another luxury, and finally got a full night's sleep.

They were entertained, too, by both movies and a USO show. The show took place on a 6 by 6 truck parked several hedgerows back. A small piano sat on the back. It was raining, and a canvas tarp covered the front half of the truck bed to keep the piano and pianist dry. Unfortunately, it didn't extend all the way to the rear of the platform that comprised the "stage." An attractive young woman named Dinah Shore appeared to sing for them. Milo was quite familiar with her. She had become quite well known, and was his father's favorite singer. She stood on the tailgate and began her performance. Soon the rain ruined her hairdo and caused her makeup to run down her face. She ignored her appearance and told the audience, "I'll stick around as long as you guys will." Milo thought she probably assumed the troops would go back to their tents to get out of the drizzle, but they were used to rain by this time. They put their helmets on the ground and sat on them. They called them an infantryman's chair because whenever there was a lull in combat, they'd sit on them and rest for a while. The GIs loved the show and nobody left. Miss Shore stuck it out with them and sang a variety of songs. Milo admired both her tenacity and her talent.[2]

Other benefits of being in reserve included receiving mail from home, a treat that didn't happen often. They also got copies of *Stars and Stripes*, the newspaper put out by the government for military personnel, and read it avidly to find out how the war was going. That might sound strange, given they were the people doing the actual fighting, but all they knew was the little world they occupied, most often a small pasture surrounded by tall hedgerows. They usually had no idea where they were. Division and regimental headquarters were generally in a town or city, but riflemen were most often out in the sticks, sometimes miles away from HQ. *Stars and Stripes* broadened their knowledge of the war's progress in Europe and in the Pacific Theater. But while the GIs enjoyed a lot of comforts that week, they still had to endure more training and marching, which they didn't appreciate at all. Given the other advantages of the leave, though, it wasn't too steep a price.

When their rest period ended the men got orders to return to the line, and were shuttle-marched through Saint-Lô, heading south. The 29th Division was to be part of a large breakthrough in German lines planned for the region of la Denisière, four or five miles south of Saint-Lô. Their first major battle was July 28th in a Saint-Lô suburb. A few days later, they faced fierce combat at Percy-du-Vier, about fifteen miles further south.

After one long, brutal struggle, Milo's unit had taken a strategic hill. Germans counterattacked, and the Americans wound up on the top of the slope surrounded by their enemy. The two forces battled for several days and before long, the GIs ran out of food and water. There were apple trees all around, so GIs ate the best apples they could pick off the trees. Eventually, they got to eating the wormy ones, and finally wound up gathering even the less-appealing fruit lying on the ground. Thirst was becoming a real problem. While apples supplied some fluid, the troops needed more. Improvising again, they drained the water out of the jackets on their .50 caliber machine guns and made it into a sort of "apple-ade." That helped with hydration for a while but left the machine guns inoperative. Without water to cool their barrels, they would quickly overheat and be ruined. Again, American ingenuity came to the fore. The problem was solved by having the men urinate into the guns' jackets. The substitute cooling fluid worked well enough, but when the weapons fired and the barrels heated up, the odor was something difficult to describe.

An American battalion finally broke through from the rear after several tries and routed the Germans so Milo's unit could leave the hilltop. Just as he began his way down the slope, German artillery opened up against the hill, firing screaming mimis. These were shells that whistled or screamed as they flew through the air. They were unnerving under any conditions, but Milo was exhausted, hungry, thirsty, and hadn't slept for several days. He was experiencing intense fear, genuine terror, and he got mad. After all he'd been through the past few days, and now the krauts were shooting at him again, using those damned scary shells. It was more than he could take, and he started running down the road, tears forming in his eyes. At the base of the hillside was a crossroads. A colonel stood there watching and called to him.

"Where are you going, son?" he asked. Milo knew he shouldn't be running; American soldiers were trained in other ways to retreat or avoid harm. He stopped and faced the officer, expecting to be chewed out. What the colonel said to him next was wonderfully comforting, something like "What are you scared of? Nothing to worry about." He also said, "You're a sergeant, son; I know how frightened you are, but you can't let your men see you running like that. It sets a bad example."

The words were effective, Milo calmed down, and went back to the front to resume fighting. Later that night, he got a little sleep, but it wasn't restful. He dreamed he was in a pasture full of Germans and could hear Panzer tanks approaching. He yelled out loud in his sleep, "They're attacking, they're attacking!" It woke up GIs sleeping near him who were, to say the least, unhappy with him. The next day other troops were "on his ass quite a bit," as Milo put it. His first sergeant really went after him, but only one officer chewed him out, so he felt it wasn't a disaster.

Before and during the battle for Saint-Lô there had been close air support (CAS) from US Army Air Force pilots flying P-47 Thunderbolts. These were single-engine fighter-bombers carrying a 500-pound bomb and four .50 caliber machine guns on each wing. When a forward observer (FO) called in an air strike, the planes would drop their bombs and strafe the enemy. Unfortunately, their efforts were often inaccurate. To delineate strike zones, GIs carried rolled up red, orange, and white cloth panels about four by eighteen feet in size. Each time a new front line was established they would unroll the panels and spread them out in front of them so pilots could see where friendly units were positioned. The system did not work effectively. FOs were far behind the targets, couldn't see them well, and thus couldn't direct the pilots accurately. Also, the pilots often couldn't see the panels through the smoke and dust created by battle. Sadly, many American soldiers were killed and wounded by their own Air Force.

Infantry commanders were furious and demanded changes. After Saint-Lô, all forward observers were Air Force lieutenants, fighter pilots themselves. Each brought along his own radioman with his radio in a backpack. Pilots were required to take FO duty in rotation, and they dreaded it. Instead of being comfortably behind the lines when not in the air, these men were now required to be right on the front hedgerow, close to all the shooting. That gave them a clear vision of the territory, and as experienced combat pilots, they were skillful at spotting targets and directing the planes. Despite their discomfort, friendly fire incidents all but disappeared, and CAS became much more effective.

German troops retreated from the Saint-Lô area in haste and fought hard to prevent the Allies from catching up to them. They knew they were losing the war in France and wanted to get back to their native country to defend it. It was mid-summer, tropically hot, and besides being perilous, the work of war was dirty, dusty, and sweaty. Milo got hit again. A German sniper had E Company pinned down and killed all the officers and non-coms except him. He was lying on the ground, and the sniper fired a round that struck the dirt and stones right in front of his face. A little piece of the bullet flew up and embedded itself in his lip, adding to the several mementos he'd carry around for the rest of his life. It surprised him how many men, including himself, were being struck by small arms fire. Before now, he hadn't thought much about rifle bullets. Artillery inflicted most of the casualties he'd seen, and that was what he'd always worried about most.

While Milo was still smarting from his sore lip, his CO ordered him out into the next field. Even though he was a sergeant, he was still acting as 1st scout, still believing the odds of not getting hit were better in that role. But having just been shot, and perhaps now doubting his own theory, he decided he'd had enough. He told the captain he wasn't going out there again. That sparked an argument between them, but before Milo got into serious trouble, a sergeant named Lee volunteered to go. He went over the hedgerow, advanced into the pasture, and nobody shot at him. Milo felt ashamed, gathered up his courage, and dashed out after the man. Within minutes, they came upon a squad of Germans running away. Milo figured the sniper who shot him was likely in the group. He emptied his M1 at them, but didn't see anyone fall. He and Lee pursued the enemy over the next hedgerow and found more Germans, who also ran off. Milo thought most or all of them got away. It was a disappointing attack, but it turned out to be significant to Milo: it was his last firefight in Normandy.

The Allies had taken Vire after ten days of intense fighting. The 116th was ordered to occupy the city and defend it against counterattacks. But on August 15th, the regiment was relieved of those occupational duties and left the next day for a week of R and R. Again, they received showers and clean uniforms, got mail, saw USO shows, and had the luxury of sleeping all night in tents. Unfortunately, their stay was cut short. General Eisenhower decided the City of Brest in Brittany had to be taken at once. While most American soldiers would continue fighting eastward toward Germany, the 29th and several other infantry divisions were assigned to General Patton's Third Army for the Brest offensive. The group was ordered to get there in time to take make an attack on the port on August 23rd.

Brittany is a historical province and a peninsula just west of Normandy that juts out into the North Atlantic. The seaport of Brest is its largest city, located on the peninsula's northwest corner. Germans had occupied it and controlled its large port facilities since the war began. It was the site of their submarine pens: huge covered docks used to house U-boats and protect them from air attacks. Built in 1941, the pens were so resistant to Allied bombs they had been largely ignored since 1942. The Allies wanted to destroy them, of course, but the primary motive for attacking Brest was to gain use of the harbor. Several seaports the Allies had counted on using after D-Day had not become available. General Eisenhower wanted another location to bring in the massive amount of materiel needed to support the forces under his command.

Chapter 10

Needless Carnage

The men of the 29th were not happy to have their rest period cut off after only four days. However, they were told taking Brest would be easy, and that the Germans there were just waiting to surrender. *Stars and Stripes* reported in August 1944 that Brest had already been captured and its port would now be available. It also said the Allied soldiers in Europe would be going home shortly or be part of the Army occupying a defeated Germany. The men's spirits were high despite their disappointment at losing several days of rest. Unfortunately, *Stars and Stripes* had it entirely wrong. Weeks earlier, Allied armor had traveled through the peninsula on its way to the Brest area, but had driven past most villages and settlements, often at twenty miles per hour. They never went into towns and secured them; that was left for the infantry. And the enemy in Brest was not about to surrender without a fight. Crack German troops were defending the city and its outlying areas. There were two large arcs of defenses around the city to protect it from invasion. Somewhere between 30,000 and 50,000 German soldiers were in the area, and many were the dreaded Nazi SS. It wouldn't be the walk in the park the newspaper predicted.

The orders General Gerhardt received gave his division only two days to move thousands of troops and all their weapons and equipment close to 250 miles over narrow, winding country roads. It was a massive operation. Hundreds of deuce and a half (2 1/2 ton) trucks were assigned, each to carry 25 men and haul a one-ton cargo trailer. Each battalion would travel in its own convoy of about 35 trucks, and for safety, would have to stop each night at 9 p.m. A recon troop of 155 men went ahead to check and clear the route. The 116th Regiment led the convoy, leaving on the evening of the 21st. The motorcade went southwest to the City of Rennes and then headed northwest toward Brest. Once the whole division got underway, the column of vehicles was over forty miles long.

Brittany is quite like its neighbor, Normandy, in many respects. It has the same climate, crops, and hedgerow-encircled pastures. It's quite different, however, in its history and culture. Vikings invaded and conquered parts of France in the ninth and tenth centuries. Many of those Norsemen (Normans) and their descendants stayed in one locale (Normandy) and settled down to lives of farming and commerce. Brittany, right next door, had been conquered three hundred years earlier by Bretons who came from England. Their culture differed greatly from Normandy and the rest of France. Their language was more like Welsh, or Cornish. They stood apart from other Frenchmen and were strongly independent. That showed in their vigorous resistance to German occupation and eagerness to help the Allies, while French leadership had easily capitulated to the Nazis.

The GIs saw little evidence of war as they entered Brittany, with citizens still living there in their undamaged homes. People massed along the roads to cheer for their liberators, giving them wine and food, and providing helpful information about enemy locations and strengths. But as the convoy got closer to Brest, German occupation became more obvious, and local people stayed in the background for their own safety.

By August 23rd, the entire 29th Division was about ten miles northwest of Brest, near the town of Saint-Renan. The next night the 116th Regiment moved to the line of departure and began its attack on the afternoon of the 25th. By August 27th, the 116th's 2nd Battalion, Milo's unit, had captured and cleared the town of Plouzané, and pushed ahead. On the morning of the 29th, they attacked La Trinité, with Milo's battalion taking the lead. They met incredible resistance from the Nazis and suffered terrible casualties. By 5 p.m., even with help from other units, the Americans had advanced only 500 yards. Things went no better the next day. General Gerhardt realized his men were exhausted and needed rest, and gave the whole division a day off on the 31st.

Milo's regiment attacked again on September 1st and 2nd and once more advanced only about 500 yards. Gen. Gerhardt ordered a unit of Rangers to help, and they knocked out some artillery that had been holding the regiment in check. Still, on September 3rd the fatigued 116th couldn't get any farther than another couple of hundred yards. The general ordered them to stand down on September 4th and planned to let the men rest. But that evening he received reports the German line was falling apart, and despite his men's fatigue, moved to take advantage of the enemy's weakness. He ordered a night assault on La Trinité, an unusual, difficult, and dangerous tactic. It worked, though, and Americans took over the area. The Germans, true to their usual practice, counter-attacked around 5 p.m. on September 5th. The battle to defend their recent acquisition continued for Milo until Gerhardt finally pulled his decimated battalion off the line on September 10th. But this break was not for rest and recreation; the men had to continue aggressive patrolling while off the front for the next four days.

It didn't take long for GIs, especially newer replacements, to realize the German troops they were facing here were much more aggressive than most they had previously encountered. There were vicious counterattacks and much hand-to-hand fighting. The Americans understood why when they found out they were facing the 2nd SS Paratroopers, an elite Nazi unit that had been in Italy in the bloody battle at Casino. These were not the typical German citizen-soldiers, many of them boys and old men. They were not people from other countries who were captured and impressed into service, many unable to speak German, ready to surrender gladly if they could do so without being shot by their German superiors. The Nazi paratroopers the GIs faced in Brittany were staunch followers of Adolph Hitler and his henchmen. They had been fully indoctrinated in Nazi beliefs and brainwashed to idolize Hitler when they were young boys in the Hitler Youth Corps. They were tough, highly disciplined, and motivated. Even after being captured, they displayed the haughty, insolent demeanor so often depicted in war movies, honoring their pledge to never surrender, to fight to the last bullet. Milo had fought men like this in Normandy and knew how dangerous they were. He described them as vicious and well trained. Tougher than nails, he said, like 15,000 rattlesnakes. Allied casualties from small arms fire increased substantially. But there was at least one improvement from the GI's point of view: the Nazis weren't using self-propelled 88s, the big guns that had terrorized them throughout Normandy.

As noted, there were apple trees all over Normandy and Brittany, and almost everywhere the troops went, lots of apples lay on the ground. If your foot landed on one, it sometimes made a popping noise. So did certain German land mines the GIs often encountered. Germans called them S-Mines, but to the Americans, they were Bouncing Betties. They consisted of a small round glass or wooden case (to avoid detection with magnets) containing ball bearings or other shrapnel. Stepping on one set off a small charge that made a popping sound, like that made by treading on an apple. That charge caused the mine to fly up three or four feet in the air where it exploded. It shot steel in all directions, and at that height, shrapnel hit men in their lower torso or upper legs. It was common for these bombs to blow one or both legs off, and/or castrate the unlucky soldier. They were designed to maim rather than kill, and were terribly frightening to the troops. As one can imagine, hearing the popping sound from stepping on an apple made the men crazy. Milo often saw groups of GIs jumping around trying to avoid an explosion in case the noise came from a mine and not a piece of fruit.

German soldiers in the Brest region were heavily dug in, protected by pillboxes, barbed wire, tank traps, and minefields.

They had taken over several centuries-old fortresses in the area and seized a huge rampart, or earthworks, called the Great Wall of Brest. It was ancient, having been there since Romans built it as one of the walls of a fortress shortly before AD 300. The rest of the building is long gone, but the one wall remained. It was roughly fifty feet high and twenty feet wide, with holes in it, tunnels going through it, roads leading up and down its sides, and buildings and a roadway along its flat top. Milo thought it looked like the Great Wall of China.

As his unit neared the structure, the 116th's Regimental Commander summoned Milo for a meeting. It wasn't often that highly ranked officers asked advice of their enlisted men, but Milo was a staff sergeant, well known for having survived the first wave on D-Day and still be fighting three months later. Very few soldiers had those credentials. Most officers and men then in the field were newer replacements, and few had his experience, knowledge, perspective, and judgment. Having a resource like Milo available was a great asset to a commander.

The colonel asked Milo whether he thought his men could take the wall. Milo said he'd take a look at it. He and two men from his platoon started up the ramp leading to the top, with the colonel watching their progress through binoculars. A white flag was suddenly thrust out of a hole in the wall and out came a rush of Germans with their hands raised. There were hundreds of them; they could easily have overpowered the three GIs, but clearly just wanted to give up. Milo was optimistic; he thought this might be a sign German troops were ready to collapse. He soon found out these prisoners were not the tough Nazi infantrymen he'd been facing in battle. They were cooks and quartermasters and even some navy men. Their surrender was not the omen he hoped for, but he was still understandably proud. The regimental CO had placed trust in him, and within half an hour he came back with at least 300 prisoners. He was awarded another Bronze Star for his efforts.[1]

Milo's rank at this time, staff sergeant, raises an interesting point. He'd been promoted twice to reach that rank, but didn't even remember the occasions. His first promotion was from buck private directly to sergeant; he never held the ranks of private first class or corporal. Later he was made a staff sergeant. Those promotions occurred during combat, and there weren't any ceremonies involved. Likely they resulted from death or injury suffered by a commanding NCO or officer, when the vacant position had to be filled by someone. Rank wasn't that important to infantrymen. Some got promoted and never put the chevrons (stripes) on their sleeves to show their new status. Others drew stripes on their uniforms with pencils. Officers and non-coms didn't want Germans to be able to identify them, so there was little recognition of rank evident. More important than rank was the position one held, or had to take over as others got wounded or killed. Most infantrymen didn't pull rank on others for the sake of ego trips. They had more important things to worry about, like staying alive and getting their jobs done.

Soon after his successful recon trip to the Great Wall, Milo received a new assignment. His unit had reached Recouvrance, a community abutting Brest on the west, very close to the harbor and the U-boat pens. His CO wanted to know how far they could advance toward the port without meeting resistance. Milo led a three-man recon patrol to find out. One of the men who went with him was a sergeant from the 3rd Platoon named Ritter. The other was a cook, not an infantryman. He apparently volunteered for the patrol because he was quite a drinker and wanted to find a bottle of good French brandy.

The trio set out through rural areas, at one point reaching a church with a high spire, a building Milo recognized from a prior patrol. They kept on into the city, seeing no enemy, and came up to a large boulevard. There was a huge bomb crater in the roadway where it intersected with a cross street. As they moved up toward the corner, they heard machine-gun fire from what sounded like an American .50 caliber gun. They went forward to see if it was Americans firing or a gun the Germans had captured (it turned out to be the latter). They spotted Nazi paratroopers approaching and, to avoid being seen, jumped into the crater. It was so deep that when Milo stood up, the street level was over his head. When on patrol, if experienced soldiers hid in a depression or hole for safety, each man watched in a different direction so they covered all points of the compass. The three men in Milo's patrol should each have been scanning 120 degrees to see if anyone was coming. Riflemen instinctively covered for everybody else in their unit. Unfortunately, the cook either didn't know that or was careless. A startled Milo heard a voice say "Hands up." He turned, and there was a German soldier behind him with a submachine gun taking them prisoner.

The three Americans were taken down several flights of stairs below the street into a subterranean tunnel about the size of a New York subway. It ran through the hill above them, connecting the two harbors of Brest. A flatbed railway car pulled by a donkey was transporting boxes of ammo from one harbor to the other without exposing it to open air. Milo could see piers with ships docked on both sides. Roughly twenty other American prisoners were there, too. Sometimes the GIs were ordered to help push the rail car, but they spent most of their time above on the boulevard, shoveling fill into bomb craters. That night they were fed meat and sauerkraut and ordered to sleep in the tunnel next to the tracks. They were questioned, but not extensively. Their shoulder patches told who they were, and these Germans were after manual labor, not information. They needed the roads repaired so they could move their tanks and other equipment. The next morning, the prisoners went back above ground, and with pickaxes and shovels filled more craters. Milo noted they were on the outskirts of town, as there were few houses, and lots of wooded, undeveloped land around.

As they worked, American P-47 planes appeared above, maneuvering for an attack. The pilots couldn't know there were GIs below and assumed all the men were Germans repairing their own roads. The planes began a strafing run, and all the American prisoners except Ritter and Milo jumped into the ditch along one side of the road, together with two German guards. Milo, Ritter, and one German guard dove into the ditch on the opposite side. That guard was wearing a paratrooper's gray woolen cap and no helmet. As the airplanes came around for a second run, Ritter hit the guard in the head with his shovel and killed him. Milo and Ritter took off running, dodging the P-47's bullets, hoping to get away before the other Germans discovered their dead comrade.

They made it to a wooded area with lots of brush and hid there until dark. It didn't appear anyone was looking for them, so they decided to try to get back to their own lines. Milo thought he could find the way because he had the tall church steeple as a landmark. They left their hideout, and despite the dark, Milo was able to retrace his steps, find the tall steeple, and wind up in the general vicinity where their unit had been when they left. As they moved into yet another field, Milo said to Ritter, "I think we're getting close."

"Halt, who goes there," he heard, along with the sound of a machine gun's bolt being cocked. Milo knew the bolt had to be pulled back twice to fire the gun, but he was scared, nevertheless. The hidden voice then gave the day's password and paused for a response. Every day headquarters assigned a new password and countersign for security purposes. A sentry challenging someone gave the current password. The other party then had to give the correct countersign or face being shot. Milo and Ritter had been gone from their outfit for a couple of days and had no idea what today's countersign was. The challenger yelled the password one more time, and said, "This is the last time I'm going to tell you." The two men heard the second click of the machine gun bolt and knew they were in deep trouble.

Milo yelled out, "I don't know what it is today, but I know what it was two days ago."

The voice in the dark said, "Oh geez, its Flaten." The sentry had been stationed there to await the return of a different patrol. Luckily, he recognized Milo's voice, and no harm was done—other than a good scare for the two returning sergeants. Milo's luck had prevailed again, both in escaping from the enemy and avoiding harm when he returned. Yet he was humiliated at having been a taken prisoner and didn't want anyone to know about it. In his opinion, any soldier who allowed himself to be captured by the enemy was an extreme embarrassment.[2]

On September 13th, the 29th Division marched back to the front lines to take part in an all-out attack on Brest. The 116th Regiment was in the center, the 115th on one side and the 175th on the other. Milo's Battalion was assigned to take Recouvrance, the last Nazi holdout. They fought there for four days, including a battle at one of the old French forts, called Keranroux. It was extremely difficult fighting, and to gain footholds the Allies used vehicles called Crocodiles. They were regular British tanks armed with flamethrowers and towing trailers holding the weapon's fuel. They were invaluable in breaching the walls of the fortresses, but still, the fighting was bitter and deadly. The GIs were once again facing ruthless, arrogant SS Nazis. When captured, they wouldn't surrender until Americans put guns in their faces and threatened to shoot.

Once they took the fort, Milo's company (now down to twelve men) went back in reserve for several days while the battle continued. It was still in reserve on September 17th when the rest of the 116th reached the bluffs overlooking the Bay of Brest. The Americans finally had control of the city, and the next day the Germans there formally surrendered. Much celebrating occurred thereafter, with GIs consuming a great deal of wine and cognac liberated from the Germans' plush quarters. They drove German vehicles around and rode the Germans' horses. But the victory, achieved at great cost in human life, was essentially meaningless. The Germans had destroyed the port facilities of Brest before surrendering, and by battle's end, another port had been repaired that was preferable. The Allies never used Brest for re-supply.

On the 19th the 29th Division's troops moved about 25 miles west to a rest area on the Le Conquet Peninsula, near a couple of quaint villages. Each contained shops, bars, restaurants, and even women: not only local residents, but American nurses and Red Cross personnel. General Gerhardt wanted his men to focus entirely on pleasure for the two weeks they planned to stay there. In fact, there were reports the general had even established an "officially" sponsored house of ill repute there he called the Blue and Gray Riding Academy. Some said Gerhardt was concerned there might be rapes if the men had no other outlet. True or not, word got out to the public and Army brass, and caused quite a scandal. A high-ranking chaplain spoke out strongly about the issue and publicly took the general to task. If such a facility existed, it was for a very short time.

Unfortunately, the war was not going well for the Allies in Germany; more troops were needed there. On September 24, after only five days of R and R, the 29th got the call. The men broke camp, got into the familiar deuce-and-a-half trucks, and left Brittany.

Chapter 11

Das Rheinland

U pon reaching Rennes, some trucks continued forward carrying their passengers to their destinations. About half of them, however, including those transporting Milo's division, were unloaded and the men were marched to waiting troop trains. The cars they boarded were like boxcars on American freight trains, but only about half as wide and half as long. These were the same cars that had been used to move soldiers around during World War I. A sign on the side of each car said "hommes 40, chevaux 8," indicating each car could hold 40 men or eight horses. Troops in World War I called them 40 et 8's, and GIs still used the name. The cars might have held forty men, but all forty couldn't sit down at the same time. They had to take turns standing and sitting throughout the length of their ride, which turned out to be nearly 500 miles. The cars were unheated and rickety; it was a miserable trip.

As the train rode through the Paris railroad yards, Milo and his mates discovered they could see the Eiffel Tower in the distance. They made another discovery there too: besides American soldiers the train was hauling large containers filled with wine. Enlisted men waited until there were no officers around and shot holes in the tanks, draining wine into the five-gallon canisters they used for carrying water. It's not hard to imagine the journey became a little easier from that point on.

Once in Belgium, the locomotive shifted cars around so different units could go to their assigned areas. All of the 29th Division except the 116th Regiment was released from offensive action and sent to Valkenburg in the Netherlands for training. Milo's regiment went to Germany, directly to the front, in an area called the Rhineland. This was originally a part of Germany straddling the Rhine River and bordering France, Belgium, and the Netherlands. It had been taken from Germany at the end of WWI by the Treaty of Versailles, and maintained as a neutral zone to prevent Germany from becoming belligerent again in the area. Hitler had nevertheless sent his troops to enter the zone in 1936 and had occupied it since.

E Company wound up near the small town of Teveren, two miles or so from the Netherlands border, and just a mile and a half southwest of the German-occupied City of Geilenkirchen. The terrain here was dramatically unlike that of Normandy or Brittany. There were no hedgerows; the land was flat and barren. Except for a few occasional trees, nothing obstructed one's view. Milo could easily see church steeples and smokestacks in Nazi-occupied Geilenkirchen. The setting was bleak: it was chilly, the skies were usually gray, and it often rained. German residents had vacated their houses, and white sheets hung from front windows indicating the Allies had appropriated them. Sadly, GIs weren't allowed to stay in them, though they did go in and check for souvenirs.

Soon after arriving, Milo was ordered out as a sniper, although he'd had no training or experience in that position. They issued him the usual sniper weapon, a 1903 Springfield .30-06 caliber bolt-action rifle with a telescopic sight—the same gun used by American soldiers in World War One. Springfields were slower and more complicated to fire than M1s. The bolt had to be pulled back and forth before each shot to eject the spent shell and chamber a new one. But they also had an advantage: while M1's were effective at between 400 and 600 yards, the '03, as they commonly called the Springfield, could hit a target up to 1,000 yards away.[1]

They sent Milo forward to an area near F Company's location, closer to Geilenkirchen than his own company's position. He walked there across acres of flat, open fields.

Milo's locations Oct. 6 through approximately Nov. 30, 1944

German spotters in Geilenkirchen easily saw him, and lobbed a few mortar shells his way, but they didn't come close. His orders were to shoot any Germans he saw, but he wasn't sure how he was supposed to do that. He'd seen a training film in boot camp where a sniper positioned himself in a tree for better visibility and decided to try that. With his M1 slung on his back and the Springfield in hand, he climbed one of the few nearby trees and got as comfortable as he could in its branches. He scoured the countryside for a considerable time, but never saw a German. When nature called, he climbed down from the tree, dropped his trousers, and squatted. Though the Germans were short on ammunition, the target was apparently too tempting. They fired a mortar round that missed Milo but hit the nearby tree. It splintered when the shell exploded, sending many small slivers of wood into his neck and face. Although he was bleeding extensively, the wounds were superficial, and he looked much worse than he felt. He pulled up his pants, went back to F Company bunker, and asked for a medic. The guys there said their medics were in Holland for training. One of them called E Company and told them their sniper had been hit and needed aid. E Company sent a jeep and a medic who bandaged Milo's face and then drove him back to the E area.

Each company had its own clerk based at Regimental Headquarters who kept the unit's records. It had been so quiet at HQ since they arrived in Germany that E Company's clerk had gone out to Teveren to catch up on the latest paperwork. When he arrived, he saw Milo with all the bandages on his face and, without talking to him, recorded that he'd been wounded. As a result, Milo received another purple heart, though he didn't learn about it until quite a while later. He was a bit amused, thinking about the circumstances.

Since D-Day, it had been the norm that all units were below strength. Though the Army continuously sent up replacements, the number of casualties was always greater. It was common for a company allotted 193 men to have only 20 or 30, less than a full-strength platoon. When the Allies got to Germany their commanders realized the push needed to defeat the Nazis would take maximal forces and fresh troops, so they poured in replacements. Most of those men were green. Not only were they without combat experience, their basic and advanced training in the States had been shortened. Little effort was made to see they were qualified before shipping them to the front. There were horror stories of tanker replacements, for instance, who had never seen or touched a tank or even learned to drive a car. Infantrymen were likewise inadequately prepared. The Army's policy had become a numbers game. Those in charge apparently decided with enough warm bodies they could simply overpower the enemy. Regrettably, many soldiers died because of their meager training, and those who survived had a tough time accomplishing their objectives.

On Friday, October 13th, replacements arrived at E Company. Milo was relieved to have a nearly full-strength platoon for the first time since before the Normandy landing, even if they were raw rookies. And it actually was *his* platoon: he'd been named platoon leader, a position normally held by a lieutenant. In fact, by then all of E Company's platoon leaders were sergeants. A Lt. Hartley was the company commander and the only officer in the unit. Milo's assistant platoon leader was a staff sergeant named David Rathke, from Columbus, Ohio. They eventually became good friends; Milo thought Dave was quite a nice guy.

The night the replacements arrived, Milo's company, along with others, was ordered to attack Geilenkirchen. There were many German pillboxes on the city's outskirts, all part of a supposedly impenetrable protective structure. Hitler called it The Siegfried Line, a cluster of defensive buildings and walls he had built between 1938 and 1940 near the German border. It stretched almost 400 miles from the Netherlands to Switzerland. Pillboxes were used to conceal troops and keep them safe while firing at their enemy. They were made of reinforced concrete and were very hard to penetrate with regular artillery. The GIs went out that night with shaped charges called beehives (after their appearance), which were much more effective. The charges were placed on top of pillboxes, and when they exploded their main force was transmitted directly down upon the concrete, rather than being sent out in all directions.

Milo assembled his platoon on the outskirts of Teveren in inky blackness and sent out the 1st scout (Milo was no longer filling that slot) with a phone set attached to a wire about 1,000 feet long. When the scout reached the end of the wire, he was to call in and report whether he had encountered any enemy. If not, the others would advance, following the wire forward to the scout's position. The scout would set out again as far as the line allowed, and if all was safe, the rest would once again advance to him. After making six or seven of those movements, Milo and his troops had traveled forward more than a mile toward enemy lines.

When the scout went out the next time Milo waited for his call, but it never came. He told Sgt. Rathke to follow the line out and see what had happened. Again, there was no call. He instructed his platoon to hunker down where they were, and took off forward, following the wire. When he reached its end, Rathke was there and okay, but the platoon's 1st scout had been killed. Dave said the scout was already dead when he got there, and the krauts had cut the wire. While they mulled over the situation, a flare went up from German lines illuminating the landscape. Then more flares rose, and German machine guns began firing. The Germans had established a line of resistance to the area they were holding, what was called a Final Protective Line. (Allies did the same thing.) They set machine guns at either end of that line, aimed at angles so their fire intersected at a point some distance out in front of them. Anyone trying to advance toward the Final Protective Line would encounter a virtual wall of bullets.

Milo and Dave were between the machine guns and the rest of their platoon, which was about a thousand yards back. They quickly flopped on the ground and began crawling off the battlefield as best they could. Both made it out without injury and returned to their company area in Teveren. When they arrived, they were told their entire platoon, over thirty men, including all the new replacements, had been killed. The crossfire of the two machine guns happened to intersect exactly at the spot where Milo had left them, and all were mowed down before they could escape. The two sergeants who survived were understandably shaken. It was an accidental catastrophe no one could have foreseen, but it disturbed Milo greatly. Even the fact it happened on a Friday the thirteenth spooked him. A report of the tragedy printed in *29 Let's Go*, the Division's newsletter, made Milo sound heroic for having survived the massacre. He read it and was ashamed. "All I did was hit the dirt," he said.

E Company's CO was killed a little later, and Battalion promoted Milo to tech sergeant and appointed him Company

Commander. From then on, T/Sgt Milo Flaten attended battalion HQ meetings, hobnobbing with captains, majors, and colonels. It was a strange situation, but officer replacements never came and someone had to do the job.

Regiment held the 2nd Battalion in reserve until October 6th, when it and the 1st Battalion were sent south to the vicinity of Kerkrade in the Netherlands. While there, Milo and Dave Rathke shared a pup tent, at one point camping next to a church. One night a thunderous noise woke them, and they looked out to see what had caused it. A huge German cannon shell was half-buried in the ground about five feet from their tent. Germans often fired their artillery at random with no target in mind, just to keep the Allies from getting comfortable. Not only did the shell in question just miss them, it didn't explode. The Flaten luck was holding strong.

Milo's company was motored west for an hour or so to Alsdorf, and then three or four miles south to the northern outskirts of Würselen, a city still held by the Germans. It was part of a force being amassed to close the so-called Aachen gap. The City of Aachen, from which the "gap" got its name, was about four miles southeast of Würselen. It was part of the Siegfried Line, and while not militarily important, was critical psychologically. It was the first stronghold on German soil attacked by the Allies, and a German defeat there would be a major blow to the Nazi cause. There had been fighting all around Aachen since September, and the Allies were floundering. XIX Corps was assigned to take the city, with the 1st and 30th Divisions in the forefront and the 29th protecting the 30th's flank.

They began by attacking Würselen but got nowhere because of heavy artillery fire directed at them. They moved south against Aachen itself, taking part in one of the fiercest battles of the war. It was house-to-house street fighting, with Germans popping up from sewer manholes and much hand-to-hand combat. Both sides incurred terrible casualties: Americans alone lost over 5000 soldiers killed or wounded. On October 21st, GIs took the center of the city and the last German garrison surrendered. Meanwhile, the 116th had been ordered back to attack Würselen again. It did so on the

20th, and by the next day the city had fallen. Milo had been in the thick of the entire campaign.

On the 23rd and 24th of October, the 116th pulled back from the line to an assembly area north of Würselen for more training. They were there to prepare for what some optimists were saying might be the last battle of the war. The old veterans weren't happy about more drills, but with the lack of experience and substandard training most replacements had received, it was more than necessary. As usual, conditions were not pleasant. November was cold and rainy, with almost solid cloud cover. Without sunshine, there was little evaporation and the land remained wet and muddy. It was also a time of nervous waiting as the men didn't know when they'd have to return to combat. They did know, though, the battle plan was to fight through the fields and small towns ahead, and capture the city of Jülich, about 12 miles northeast.

Orders eventually came down, and on November 16th the regiment began its attack across open ground, moving towards Aldenhoven, a city on the way to Jülich. It was a ferocious battle. Germans were defending their homeland and fought savagely. GIs tried using scouts and fire and maneuver, but that didn't work. The Americans were completely exposed on the bare flat land with nowhere to hide, while the Germans were invisible in their foxholes.

After several days of continuous heavy fighting, Milo noticed one of his sergeants was crying and had succumbed to battle fatigue. He went to the man and started guiding him back to the command post where the first sergeant was located. Suddenly Milo crumpled to the ground. He had been hit on the top of his head by a piece of shrapnel that drove through his helmet and liner and lodged in his skull. He was unconscious from the instant of impact. Medics took him to the rear, ultimately to the 113th Evacuation Hospital about 60 miles west, close to Liège, Belgium. It was there he awoke, discovered where he was, and was told what had happened. The fragment of metal, about the size of a quarter, was still embedded in his skull, and the trauma was causing him to fade in and out of consciousness.

The facility had large tents which each held about 100 patients on their stretchers. As Milo lay there, he could hear buzz bombs—V-1 rockets—flying by. He asked a nurse about them, and she said he could go outside and watch them if he wished. Medics carried him out and he found he was up on a hill with a wide panorama. He was fascinated to watch V-1's fly past toward the city of Liège, about ten miles away. Allied P-51 fighter planes were there too, chasing the buzz bombs and trying to shoot them down. The rockets were so slow Milo thought it was like watching Piper Cubs fly. As they neared the city their engines stopped, and they slowed even further. Finally, they nosed over and dove to the ground, causing an enormous explosion when they hit. Observing it all from his vantage point, it seemed unreal to Milo; somewhat like watching a movie.

After a while, with his head swathed in bandages, medics loaded him onto a C-47 (a DC-3 in the civilian world) and he was flown to Christchurch, England, right next to Bournemouth. Milo was one of many wounded lying on banks of stretchers all over the plane. He didn't remember either taking off or landing, but was conscious for much of the flight itself. The weather was good, the plane ride smooth, and he was in no pain; it was a comfortable trip for him. When he woke up, he was in a hospital in Christchurch in a ward with other head-wound cases. Doctors evaluated him and decided not to operate to remove the shrapnel. Milo thought maybe their decision was a result of the Army's desperate need for replacements. Most new recruits and draftees were being sent to the Pacific, as action there was becoming hotter. Or perhaps the choice was based on medical findings and judgments. Milo wasn't told the reason, but in any event, the shrapnel stayed where it was.[2]

As he lay in bed recovering, one of the hospital staff informed him there was going to be an award ceremony. Soon an officer and several soldiers came into his ward and presented him with a medal, a Silver Star. It was for his bravery in taking out the big German gun on his first day in the bocage. Captain Johnson had been so impressed by Milo, he'd nominated him for the decoration. The Silver Star was the third-highest medal awarded by the armed forces; only the Service Cross for each military branch and the Medal of Honor were higher. Milo was proud and pleased to receive it, although he wasn't that impressed with what he had done.

Within weeks Milo healed enough so he could get up and around. Still wearing head bandages, he went sightseeing in several towns: Christchurch where the hospital was located, Bournemouth, and Southampton, where he'd been before D-Day.

He didn't know it, but soon after he was injured several soldiers met with his mother at the factory where she worked in Milwaukee. They told her Milo had been captured and was presumed dead. It was a horrible message, and Winnie was overcome with grief. It didn't dawn on Milo to contact his parents until Christmas neared. He sent them a telegram on Christmas Eve saying: "Best Wishes for Christmas and New Year. Have you received letters? Love, Milo." His parents were stunned and understandably overjoyed.

He remained hospitalized until after Christmas, and happily for him, his holiday was far from bleak. An extremely nice older English couple he met invited him and another wounded GI into their home for Christmas Eve and Christmas Day. The other fellow was a sergeant named Davey Crockett, a red-haired Texas kid who claimed to be a direct descendant of his famous namesake. The two young men shared a wonderful dinner with the couple which included meat (a rare commodity in war-torn England) and slept in real, comfortable beds. It was a memorable occasion Milo thoroughly enjoyed. A few days later, his doctors declared him fully recovered and discharged him from the hospital. It was time to go back to work.

Chapter 12

A Notable Respite

Milo was taken to Bournemouth and on January 1st boarded a ship that took him across the channel to Calais. From there, he took a train to a repple depple in the ancient city of Étampes, about 50 miles south of Paris. The depot was an old French cavalry stable and not very accommodating. Men slept one to a horse stall on the concrete floor. New arrivals were given fresh uniforms and shots and were interviewed. Most questions were routine, like what outfit had you been with, and where were you wounded. Another standard question was, "Have you ever been captured?" Reluctantly Milo answered yes, but quickly added that he'd escaped. The interviewer said he'd have to go to SHAEF (Supreme Headquarters, Allied Expeditionary Force) in Paris, to be questioned by G-2, the intelligence branch. G-2 wanted to know about anything captured soldiers had seen behind enemy lines.

He took a train to Paris, where a man from G-2 met him and took him downtown to a hotel. He was checked in and taken to his room. It was a novel and interesting experience for Milo, his first stay in Paris and the first hotel room he'd ever been in. Following instructions, he took the metro (the Paris subway) to the G-2 office, met with an officer, and told the story of his capture and escape in Brest. The intelligence officer questioned him at length and then told him to go back to his hotel room and await new orders. He sat in his room for a while and waited, but got bored as the hours went by.

He was restless for some something to do, but had no valid money, just the invasion currency given the troops before they left England. He knew it was worthless now. He hadn't been paid since D-Day and doubted he would be while in Paris. Then someone told him there was an Army pay station at the Place de l'Opéra, a famous public square in the center of Paris. He still had his Army pay-book. It was filthy from going through the ocean, rainstorms, and muddy foxholes, but he cleaned it up as best he could and took it to the station. The clerk asked how much money he wanted. He knew tech sergeants earned $150 per month, but he had no idea how much was in his account. Jokingly he asked for what he thought was a huge amount and was amazed when they gave it to him. Leaving the hotel, he went out "on the town," searching for the best-looking girl he could find—but definitely not a prostitute. He met a lovely young woman who showed interest in him. They got along well, and Milo moved into her attic apartment. There was no coal for the furnace or any other way to heat the building. Though the rooms were biting cold, it seems the two managed to keep warm, and Milo never reported any complaints about the arrangement.

After more than a week in Paris, SHAEF released him and sent him back to the repple depple in Étampes. There he found out General Eisenhower had established a new regulation. Anyone who'd been wounded more than twice was not to be sent back to the front. Milo was more than qualified for the exemption, though he wouldn't have used it for himself. But against his will he was reassigned to a non-combat unit, a Military Police (MP) Battalion in Paris. He was stunned when they told him and said he didn't want to go. He told the officer in charge he hated MPs even more than he hated officers. As usual, the Army gave no consideration to his protests and sent him on his way back to Paris.

The MP battalion Milo joined was made up of nearly a thousand men divided into a variety of different specialties; it had been in Paris since August. He was assigned to what he called the morals squad, technically a Morals Platoon, and he became the platoon sergeant. At the time, there were over 13,000 registered (legal) prostitutes in Paris; every bar and hotel had its complement. In addition, Milo guessed there were more than 100,000 who were unregistered. With all the GIs stationed there plus all the men traveling through or there on leave, the women had plenty of business. The Morals Platoon was there to enforce regulations and keep the peace. If a GI got into a fight in a bar or with a prostitute, they might arrest the GI, and/or the woman, or shut down the bar. MPs also enforced registration of the women, and saw to it that any prostitute with venereal disease didn't work until re-certified as healthy by a physician. The Army was taking whatever steps it could to prevent the spread of illness. Any outbreak could decimate the ranks, which were already seriously under strength.

An MP unit like Milo's, stationed behind front lines, didn't face enemy arms and artillery as infantrymen did. It rarely lost any of its members, and consequently, there were few openings or promotions available. Some men had been in the battalion five or ten years and were still privates. Some privates and corporals in his platoon were ten to twenty years older than Milo. For a nineteen-year-old kid to be a tech sergeant in the MPs was almost unheard of. He may have been the youngest top-ranking non-com in the battalion.

They assigned him to street patrol. He was driven around in a jeep, handling complaints and emergencies just as a peacetime police officer would. Most incidents he responded to were fights. He'd check out the stories of the people involved, and if a GI was at fault, would take the man in handcuffs to the Paris Police station, Place de la Bastille. An MP there would contact the Army Detention Facility, and a member of that unit would pick up the prisoner and handle further processing.

Milo's company was housed near the Bastille in another old cavalry horse barn where men slept in bunk beds in the horse stalls. While more comfortable than the repple depple, the arrangements were far from luxurious. As soldiers have ever been wont to do, Milo occasionally complained about his living conditions. A fellow GI suggested he might want to get into a unit which boarded at the Petit Palace, a former department store. The MP Traffic detachment lived there as well as G-2 and Glenn Miller's Army Air Force band. The man said it was a much nicer place to stay. It was heated, there were showers, and it had several mess halls, including one for senior sergeants. After three weeks in the horse barn, those accommodations sounded wonderful, and Milo applied for a transfer to the traffic unit. There happened to be an opening, he was reassigned, and happily moved into the Petit Palace.

As a platoon sergeant, he managed traffic details—the men who directed traffic throughout the city. There was no electricity to run traffic lights and signals, so MPs were assigned to many of the larger intersections. This made sense since most vehicles on the streets belonged to the US Army and its Allies. Each morning Milo walked almost six miles north to the motor pool at St. Denis. There he met a driver and a 6 by 6 truck carrying a complement of MPs. They drove through the city, dropping off two soldiers at each designated intersection. Those men took turns directing traffic, two hours on, two hours off. When their shift ended, another sergeant and 6 by 6 would pick them up or bring their replacements. Most intersections were manned twelve hours a day, but the busiest were staffed around the clock. Milo planned and orchestrated his part of the operation, supervised the men under him, and kept necessary records.

Most traffic MPs carried carbines (though not while directing traffic), but Milo wore a .45 automatic pistol, just as officers did. His living arrangements were almost like an officer's, too. He and two others shared a spacious room and a bath. Milo went to the mess for tech, first, and master sergeants. It was a fancy cafeteria compared to most enlisted men's messes, and he ate very well.

He also got to meet interesting people as he waited in line to go in. One day he stood next to a somewhat older sergeant and asked the man what he did. "I'm the drummer in the Glenn Miller Orchestra," he replied. He offered his hand and said, "My name's Ray McKinley." Milo was stunned. McKinley was a well-known musician. This was the big band, or swing, era, and the Glenn Miller Orchestra was one of the most popular touring and recording groups of the time. Miller was an excellent trombonist who had played with several name bands before the war. He had then started his own orchestra, and as a gifted arranger, caused his ensemble to sound different from all the other popular bands of the day. It became hugely successful. Dance orchestras like Miller's, Benny Goodman's, and the Dorsey Brothers' were equivalent in popularity to the Beatles and Rolling Stones in their day.

When America entered the war, Miller wanted to do his part. Too old to be drafted, he volunteered his services to the military. The Navy turned him down, but the Army accepted his offer and decided to use the band to entertain troops. The Miller organization was assigned to the Army Air Force, and Miller was made a captain (and later promoted to major.) The orchestra was stationed in England, but once Paris was liberated, Miller wanted to be located there. He got the band transferred, and all its personnel and support people moved to Paris. Miller stayed behind to take care of some final business and left England to rejoin the band on December 15, 1944. He hopped a ride on a single-engine British plane headed for Paris but never arrived. Neither the occupants nor the aircraft were ever seen again, and no one ever found out what happened. Weather was terrible that day, which may have caused an accident. The plane might have been hit by bombs jettisoned from high-altitude US bombers returning to their base. Or friendly anti-aircraft fire might have shot it down by mistake. Whatever the case, there is little doubt the plane crashed into the English Channel. The death of a man of Miller's fame was a terrible loss and received a great deal of attention. He was a renowned celebrity. His records topped the charts of the day, and he had been featured in Hollywood movies. The international impact of his passing was similar in scope to the death of John Lennon many years later. Despite the tragedy, the Miller band continued to perform in Paris, playing two shows a day between movies at the Olympia Theater, a large cinema on the Champs-Élysées, the large avenue through downtown Paris.

McKinley suggested Milo check out the band's show, and the next night he attended the 10 p.m. performance. Jerry Gray ran the band now, with McKinley the front man and announcer. After the show, Milo met McKinley and some other band members, and they asked if he'd like to go out with them to visit a club. He said he would, and they told him they were headed for Montmartre. McKinley warned him it was a night club district and not a great neighborhood, but Milo knew it well from his days on the morals squad and had no qualms about going there. He offered to get a vehicle to transport them all; with his rank and status, he could check out any equipment he wished. He picked up an eight-passenger van from the motor pool and drove the men to the club. Most of the Miller musicians were older than Milo, and he probably looked boyish and naïve to them. That image was certainly shattered when the "girls" from the club saw the group coming. They clearly knew Milo, hugged him and called him by name, and welcomed him and his friends to their place.

It seems incredible that Milo, a teenaged bass player, met and befriended members of the Miller orchestra. They were some of the most talented swing musicians in the world, including pianist Mel Powell and clarinetist Peanuts Hucko. One of the trumpet players, Bobby Nichols, wasn't much older than Milo, and the two eventually became good friends. (Though his nickname was Red, he wasn't the famous jazz trumpeter and bandleader of the same name.) A fellow named Clarence Alpert, nicknamed Trigger, played string bass. The "boy" singer (as male vocalists were called in those days) was the well-known Johnny Desmond.[1] In addition, the establishment, The Hot Club, was owned and operated by gypsy guitarist Django Reinhardt,[2] then the best-known jazz musician in all of Europe[3] Not only did Milo get to hear Django in person, but he often played bass during jam sessions, some of which included Reinhardt.

There were members of the Miller band at the Hot Club almost every night. A table was reserved for them. They drank for free and they played for free. They'd often liberate food from their mess and bring it to the club where it would be cooked and served to any musicians there. After Django's band played its show, other musicians were invited to sit in and jam. Nichols was often the first, with others soon to follow. Miller band members didn't sit in every night, but when they did, McKinley brought a bass and a drum set with him. Milo sat in often, trading off with other bass players. Over time, Milo and Django became well acquainted. It was all heady stuff for a teenager from Milwaukee.

But spending almost every night at the Hot Club wasn't very convenient for Milo. The Miller musicians weren't on duty until evenings, and they could jam and party until five or six in the morning. and still get enough sleep. Milo had to be at his day job early each day, and with the schedule he was keeping was becoming sleep deprived. Django had an empty room for rent in his building above the club and suggested Milo stay there. Although it was unheated (like most of the buildings in Paris) it saved Milo the long trek to his quarters. He had only to walk upstairs to catch a few hours of sleep before work. In the morning, the truck driver would get his group of MPs on board and drive to Montmartre to pick him up. The arrangement worked well, and no one ever objected to it.

Trigger Alpert had married a local girl while the band was stationed in England, and she was about to give birth to their first child. He wanted to be with his wife for the event and requested a leave. McKinley told Jerry Gray he thought Milo could handle the bass chair in Alpert's absence, and Gray agreed. Trigger got his two-week furlough to return to England, and Milo was assigned temporary duty (TDY) with the band. For two weeks, in addition to his MP traffic duties, he played bass fiddle with the Glenn Miller Orchestra. Although he wasn't getting much sleep, he didn't care. He felt like a big shot, and others were treating him that way. During the day he made up for lost sleep by sending someone else out on the truck and grabbing catnaps when he could. As tiring as it was, he would have loved to continue that life, but Trigger returned. Milo went back to running his platoon of traffic cops and spending his nights jamming at the Hot Club.

He knew he had a pretty sweet life. Nobody was shooting at him. He had a decent bed, hot meals, and plenty of drinks. He played music with some of the best musicians in the world. He almost never had to go to bed alone unless he wanted to. But he was also uncomfortably aware that front-line infantry units in Europe were drastically under strength and weren't receiving needed replacements. Most new recruits were being readied to ship out for the invasion of Japan. To resolve the problem in Europe, the Army asked its soldiers in other specialties to voluntarily transfer to the infantry. Officers were ordered to recruit as many men as they could and were given quotas to meet. There were posters everywhere, including Milo's mess hall, appealing to GIs, and especially combat veterans, to sign up for action. It was hard for Milo not to notice. As pleasant as his life was, he was seriously entertaining thoughts of volunteering to go back to the front. He'd read in the papers that the 29th had taken deep injuries at Jülich, and he felt bad he hadn't been there to do his part. He watched GIs coming into Paris for R & R in battle dress, with branches and leaves still attached to their helmet netting. Those guys were facing death every day, and he was safe and sound, living the good life every night.

His feelings of guilt increased, and in addition to being conscience-stricken, he was sick of the MPs and tired of Paris. Most men in his outfit resented him. He was far above them in rank and many years younger. They made it obvious they didn't enjoy having him around, and he realized his comradeship with infantrymen was much more important to him. Even though he hated being in combat, it was what made him the proudest. The only medal he cared about wearing was his Combat Infantryman's Badge. He gave credit to the artillery and airmen, the truck drivers and cooks, and all the other members of the military who contributed to the effort. But to him, the guys who won a war were on the front line, facing the enemy with rifles, machine guns, knives, and fists. It was an elite group, and he wanted to be a part of it again. In the end, it wasn't a hard decision. He chose to return to the infantry — providing he could go back to his old unit.

He went to see the battalion commander and said with one

condition he'd be willing to help the officer out with his quota. He wanted a promise he'd be assigned to his original outfit: 1st Platoon, E Company, 116th Regiment, 29th Inf. Division. The CO agreed, orders were cut, and Milo began his journey from Paris back to the front at the Mönchengladbach area, deep inside Germany. He didn't know there'd be a couple of surprises awaiting him.

Chapter 13

Mopping Up

On his trip back to Germany, Milo was startled to find an error in his orders. The clerk who typed them got everything right except the regiment; he was being sent to the 1st Platoon, Company E, *175th* Infantry Regiment, 29th Division—not the 116th. His initial reaction was anger. Not that the 175th itself was somehow inferior; it was likely the oldest regiment in the Army. They called it the Dandy 5th of Maryland when General Washington was its commanding officer during the Revolutionary War. Still, historic or not, it wasn't his outfit, and it wasn't what he'd bargained for. This was a typical Army-style snafu, and it really irked him for a while. Eventually, he realized if he went back to his old company, he wouldn't know anybody there. No doubt every man would have been replaced in the three months he'd been gone. He realized it didn't make much difference which regiment he joined, and his anger soon subsided.

Something else got to him, though, an even tougher pill for him to swallow. As the war progressed, junior officers were being killed and wounded at an alarming rate, faster than the Army could replace them. To fill the ranks, the Army began offering commissions to experienced sergeants. They sent those who accepted back to a camp for several weeks of intensive instruction and then returned them to the front as 2nd lieutenants. The Army knew better than to send the newly commissioned officers back to their original outfits, so it placed them in other units where they were unknown. Milo had been offered a commission several times, but always turned it down. He was sure when the war in Europe was over most officers would have to take part in the invasion of Japan. That didn't appeal to him at all.

What he didn't know, however, was that after he was wounded and taken to England, a commission was offered to Sergeant Dave Rathke, and Dave took it. When he finished his training, 2nd Lt. Rathke was transferred from the 116th Regiment to a new unit: 1st Platoon, E Company, *175th* Regiment, 29th Division. So, on February 23rd, when Milo reported to his new outfit, he was the platoon sergeant, and Lt. David Rathke was his platoon leader. His former assistant was now his boss, and an officer to boot. Milo found having to salute him and call his old underling "sir" more than annoying. He tried talking to Dave several times, hoping to re-establish an informal friendship, but the new lieutenant wouldn't bend. Milo guessed he must have received very strict and strenuous training regarding his new position, and wouldn't deviate from it. Thereafter, the two men were less than close.

Milo decided to make a change of his own at that point. He didn't want to serve under Rathke, and he also wasn't interested in always being closest to danger. He'd quit being 1st scout long ago, but he'd still taken more than enough fire on the front lines. When an opening came up for a platoon sergeant for the weapons platoon, he applied. Those units were usually stationed considerably to the rear of the front, and that appealed to him. A weapons platoon included two .30 caliber machine gun teams, two 60mm mortar teams, and two 60mm bazooka teams. Its job was to support the three rifle platoons in its company. (There was a separate weapons company which had heavier armament: .50 caliber machine guns and 82mm mortars.) The CO asked if he'd had weapons experience, and Milo told him, "Oh, sure, lots of it." Though not exactly true, the CO bought it. However, there was another hurdle: Milo was a tech sergeant, and the position required a staff sergeant, one rank below his. Without hesitation, Milo agreed to a demotion and wound up getting the post. He'd lose a little authority and a slight amount of pay, but he'd be farther back from injury and death for the rest of the war. That meant a lot, and losing a stripe was of minimal importance to him.

When Milo joined his new unit, the city of Mönchengladbach had already been taken and was empty. The 29th went into reserve, the men moved into apartments on the outskirts of the city, and the COs kept their charges busy with more training and athletics. On March 31st, they broke camp and crossed the Rhine River, reassembling around forty miles north near a town called Dinslaken. Division HQ ordered the 115th and 116th Regiments on Displaced Persons duty, aiding refugees enslaved or forced out by the Germans. Milo's 175th Regiment was trucked 375 miles east to the area of Dresden, where it was ordered to clean out local forests.

Much of Germany, close to a third of the country, was heavily wooded. As German troops retreated, they took advantage of these forests and hid from the advancing Allies. They carried out guerilla-style warfare from behind their cover, shooting up convoys and stealing Allied provisions and materiel. One such forest was in Klotzsche, a district in the Dresden metropolitan sector. Milo and his comrades began mopping-up operations there, entering the woods in large sweeps and capturing or killing all the Germans they found. Milo hadn't heard a shot fired from the day he arrived in Germany until he reached that forest, but there his 2nd Battalion got into a tough firefight. German machine-gun fire killed one officer and one enlisted man, and the battalion pulled back. The 1st and 3rd Battalions returned the next day and completed the assignment. They also liberated large amounts of stolen food and provisions, along with Allied artillery, armor, and vehicles. Once that woods was cleared, the whole regiment was sent to clear the Forest Knesebeck, located south of Wittingen.

Milo's locations February 23, 1945, to January 1, 1946

While in that area, Milo's company was assigned to move forward to pick up some prisoners. American soldiers well knew the end of the war was near. Officers were getting lax, discipline was going out the window, and leadership suffered greatly. Probably as a result, nobody had obtained proper intelligence about this mission. What E Company found when they arrived were not POWs, but a group of holdout Nazi SS troops in no mood to surrender. There was a terrible battle, and many GIs were killed or seriously injured. It was the last combat Milo would see in World War II, and with his luck still holding, he made it through without being harmed.

On April 26th, trucks picked up the 175th Regiment and drove it to the Elbe River. It relieved another regiment, and the men settled in to await Russian soldiers advancing from the north and west. The Army ordered GIs not to go across the river and prohibited them from fraternizing with Russians once they arrived. While Russians were allies of America, our government did not trust them. Many US military and political leaders feared Russia would become our enemy after the war. Stalin's practices were not much different from Hitler's. In fact, the two countries had signed non-aggression pacts before the US entered the war, pacts which Hitler then ignored.

American troops had hoped to invade and capture Berlin to end the war; it was a point of pride for them. But because of political maneuvering, the Allies agreed to stop at the Elbe, meet the Russians there, and let the Soviets go ahead to Berlin. The decision was unpopular among Americans, both military and civilian, and it was both complicated and confusing to US soldiers. They just didn't understand the game plan. If the Russians were on our side, why were GIs supposed to treat them like an enemy? It made no sense at all.

Milo's unit was located far out in the country, probably near a little town he thought was called Damnatz, but he was unsure. A few areas along the Elbe were still receiving occasional German artillery fire and bombing, but there wasn't any combat going on in Milo's location. The only warlike noises came from a .50 caliber machine gun a couple of GIs were firing across the river. They ignited the thatched roof of a barn with tracers and watched it burn to the ground, just for something to do.

The weather was cold and rainy, and the Elbe was at flood stage. Germans had apparently opened a dam somewhere hoping to flood the Allies out. For a while after they arrived, Milo's outfit was alone, but soon German civilians and some soldiers appeared on the other side of the river, wanting to cross and surrender to Americans to avoid the approaching Russians. They knew Americans were more humane than Russians; the latter had a reputation for being rapists and brutal captors. GIs were under orders to keep Germans from reaching the Allied shore, but the Germans were tenacious and strongly motivated to get into American custody. Many swam across, some holding on to boards. Others rowed over in leaky old boats. GIs watched a lot of them drown, but never shot at them. And along with the German people crossing the river, close to thirty homeless German shepherd dogs paddled across. Milo made friends with one, named him Schnapps, and kept him as a pet.

There were only about thirty men left in Milo's platoon, and not having seen an officer for quite a while, they were becoming a very undisciplined bunch. They scrounged around old buildings in the area, found some beat-up boats, and paddled across the river, despite orders. One of the first to return reported Russians were now over there. More men made the trip, and eventually most of the platoon crossed the river, including Milo. He rowed over, got up on a dike, and could see Russians encamped nearby. He met some of them and found them quite hospitable. For about a week GIs went back and forth across the river, taking schnapps to the Russians and getting vodka back from them. They got along well, and everybody seemed to have a good time.

On May 2nd, groups of German soldiers appeared at the river bearing white flags. Russians were not far behind, shooting at them even as they tried to surrender. Most of the Germans were smiling, happy to be safe and done with the war, and gladly gave up their weapons. Occasionally officers showed up carrying Luger pistols, which GIs highly valued as souvenirs. Milo and others took the guns and stuffed them in their barracks bags to take home.

Then, despite the orders to stop Germans from crossing to the American side, GI engineers appeared and built a large pontoon bridge over the river. As soon as they completed it, US Army trucks filled with Germans crossed over. Milo couldn't understand what was going on. Eventually, someone told him: most of the passengers were rocket scientists and technicians who had been working on the German V-2 program. America wanted their knowledge and expertise available for its rocket program. For the same reason, Russia was also trying to capture as many scientists as it could, and there was a tense competition between the two nations.[1]

Around May 4th, with the war almost over, the 29th Division was shipped out to help take over occupation of a district called the Bremen Enclave. It was an area of about 1,500 square miles including the ports of Bremen and Bremerhaven, both of which the Allies wished to use for their own purposes. The area was put under joint operational control of British and American forces as matters were sorted out after the war.

The US Army began sending some of its troops back to the States even before the end of the war in Europe in preparation for the invasion of Japan. However, those who fought longest and hardest in Europe were to be rewarded with a release from further service. A point system was created which allowed men with at least eighty-five points to be sent home for discharge. Points were assigned based on various criteria, including the number of months served in the Army, the number of campaigns fought in, the number of awards received, and so on. Milo's point total came to 135, but he wasn't able to take advantage of it. He had to stay in Europe with his division as it remained on active duty as part of the military forces that would occupy the defeated country.

Germany surrendered on May 7th, Milo's 20th birthday. He hoped it would be declared the end-date of the war, but the formal ceremony was put off for a day. The 8th of May happened to be the birthday of US President Harry S Truman, who had considerably more seniority than Milo. He declared the official VE Day (Victory in Europe Day) to be on *his* birthday. Milo's 175th Regiment was still traveling that day and was located at a temporary assembly area over 100 miles from Bremen. Even though his birthday had passed, Milo celebrated on the 8th anyway—both his birthday and VE Day. He heated water, put it in a cattle trough, and took a leisurely bath. He lay there quite a while, looking up at the sky. It was the first time in months he didn't scan for warplanes.

Chapter 14

A Waiting Game

It took two weeks to move the entire 29th Division into the Bremen area. The 175th arrived on May 19th and found the location was mostly rubble. Milo's platoon was ordered to set up a perimeter defense near the docks, which turned out to be quite fortuitous for its members. They discovered a Beck's Brewery located on a dock below street level. Numerous 700-gallon cauldrons full of beer were there, which GIs immediately tapped and heartily sampled. As there were no intact bedrooms for them anywhere near, the men stayed overnight in the brewery's undamaged rathskeller. Each man kept a five-gallon can of beer next to his bedroll.

Besides all the beer, there were also large tanks nearby filled with a type of alcohol Germans used to fuel their buzz bombs. GIs were emphatically warned this kind of alcohol was not for human consumption, and if they drank it, they'd probably go blind. Some soldiers thought the warning was made up just to keep them away from booze. They had a few drinks, and some did, indeed, go blind. Milo was ordered to send one of his men to take over a home near the tanks and set up an outpost to guard the alcohol so no one else would be harmed.

In order to provide decent places for the soldiers to live, the Army kicked Germans in the village of Hagen out of their homes, and Milo's outfit moved in there for a three-week stay. He was billeted in the town's schoolhouse, which he considered adequate but sparse. Then his unit moved to Blumenthal, about sixteen miles northwest of Bremen. The accommodations there were much nicer, with the men sleeping in real beds with sheets and blankets. The town was quite modern in comparison with some little rural places they'd been.

One of the 29th Division's duties was to share in the operation of a Separation Center for German POWs. The division alternated management with a British division, with each group running the facility for two weeks at a time. The Allies wanted German soldiers discharged from their army and sent home quickly to avoid any possibility of further military action. The Center was a huge operation, with about 8,000 German prisoners staying there at any given time. Each was investigated to see whether he had been a Nazi, in the SS, or otherwise involved in the commission of war crimes. Any who had were detained for further investigation and possible charges. The rest received official documents declaring they had not been Nazis,[1] and were shipped out on cattle trains to their various homelands, mainly Germany, Austria, France, and Czechoslovakia. GIs from the Center were periodically assigned to the trains to guard the prisoners. Milo and his platoon were selected once and took a group to Innsbruck, Austria. The POWs were not treated graciously. The train didn't stop to let them get off; it only slowed down at stations, and those leaving had to jump or were pushed off.

The Allies were also concerned that civilian Germans in the area who were angry about the surrender might wage guerrilla warfare. GIs were therefore used as a constabulary, and, like a municipal police force, were charged with keeping order in the area. Each night, one company went on patrol driving jeeps with machine guns mounted on them, staffed by at least one officer and an enlisted man.

Although the GIs had various duties, they also had a lot of free time and spent much of it engaged in sports. Milo played lots of baseball and entered a swimming meet. Several (American style) football teams were formed, and he was chosen to be his team's place-kicker. He described himself as a weak kicker, and his teammates teased him by calling him Thunderfoot. He also played quite a bit of soccer. The British division stationed there had a team, and an American soccer team was organized to play against them. Not surprisingly, the GIs never won against the Brits. Football, as the English call soccer, was one of their favorite sports, and most young men had considerable experience playing it. At that time, soccer was only occasionally played in the US, mostly in gym classes, and primarily by girls, not boys. It was not a popular sport, and few Americans played it well. The Yanks' inability to beat the British team (the Dortmund Gyros) stuck in Milo's craw.

Besides sports, Milo played sousaphone in the Regimental Band and string bass in a six-piece dance band which performed at the nearby Air Force Base Officers' Club. Normally, GIs wouldn't be allowed to take a truck and leave their own base for such purposes, but Milo's CO felt there was a good reason for them to go. The only "legal" alcoholic beverage his men could buy was "near beer," which had half the alcohol content of traditional brews. Milo and his musician friends took empty canteens with them to their band jobs, and during breaks filled the flasks with Air Force booze to bring back to their buddies. It was not surprising their CO supported this manner of recreation and mode of supply for his troops. Most soldiers were drinking heavily whenever they could. Officers especially were under the influence much of the time, and Milo thought the resulting lack of discipline was appalling. One night when he was scheduled for patrol, he searched all through the Center to locate an officer sober enough to accompany him. The only one he could find was a chaplain, a Catholic priest named Father Ryan. It was a memorable night as the good Father wound up delivering a young German girl's baby. Thankfully, he was fully sober and up to the task.

After Germany surrendered, many of its soldiers were stranded in the distant countries they had been occupying. The Center was responsible for getting them back to Germany and processing their separation from their army. Men in the 175th were asked to volunteer as guards on the ships being sent over to get them. Milo did so once and boarded a boat in Bremerhaven headed for Norway. The trip over was uneventful, but Milo was a sensation when he got off the ship. The recently liberated Norwegians saw the name Flaten on his uniform and went wild. Here was one of the conquering Americans, obviously of Norwegian descent, as he had one of the most common Norwegian surnames. A celebration was in order. Milo barely remembered the party; it lasted three days and nights, and he never bought a drink or paid for food the whole time. He was celebrated as a hero and loved it.

Eventually, it came time to sober up and take command of his prisoners. When he got to their holding area he met their CO, a typically haughty German major. The man said he would not surrender his troops to someone of lower rank—and certainly not to a non-commissioned officer. Milo said he'd be okay with that. He'd just leave all the krauts there and let the Norwegians have their fun with them. That was argument enough for the major. He knew many of his men might not survive if left alone with their angry former captives. He surrendered his troops without further objection, and the Americans escorted them back to Germany. On the trip back, Milo discovered some of the POWs were experienced soccer players. He met with them and found they were happy to go along with a plan he'd been working on. The next time his soccer team played the Gyros, it included some Germans dressed in American uniforms. The Yanks finally beat the Brits at their own game.

Once all the Germans were processed and sent away, the Separation Center was used to send Allied troops home. It was Milo's turn to go in late December. He went to Bremerhaven and boarded a Liberty Ship, the City of Devonshire, which sailed for America on January 1st. Milo spent most of his time onboard playing cards, primarily poker, a game he was still learning. There were plenty of card sharks in the group, and he was soon out of money. However, there were more important matters afoot. After four days at sea, the ship ran into a violent storm which damaged it and forced it to stop. The vessel closest to them was a Canadian Corvette, a small antisubmarine patrol boat. It came to the rescue and towed their ship to Bristol, England. While there, Milo learned merchant marines were buying any Lugers the GIs wanted to sell. He still had some in the barracks bag he'd filled at the Elbe, sold them all, and was solvent again.

In Bristol, the troops boarded a Victory ship, a larger and faster class of troop carrier than the one he'd been on. While their Liberty ship would have taken twelve days to reach New York, the Victory-class vessel only took seven. Milo's earlier losses at poker had been instructive, and he now felt he understood the game. He started playing again, and by the time they made port he carried a fair amount of cash in his money belt.

As the ship entered the New York harbor, almost all the soldiers came up on deck to watch. Milo saw the Statue of Liberty passing by, but there were so many GIs crowded around the rail he had trouble seeing anything else, even with his height. He found a box to stand on and finally could see the shore. There were signs hung on almost every building bearing messages like "Welcome Home. Well Done." The roofs were filled with people clapping and waving at them. Boats in the harbor saluted them, and fireboats shot great columns of water into the sky. He felt very proud.

The soldiers disembarked and traveled by train to Camp Kilmer, New Jersey, for processing. Those without enough points for discharge were sent to the West Coast. The "older guys," as Milo called them, men like him with enough points, were to be sent to the Army post closest to their home for discharge. In Milo's case, that was Fort Sheridan in Highwood, Illinois, about 28 miles north of Chicago. After a few days at Camp Kilmer, an officer showed up and told Milo, "Get your platoon out." Once formed up, the officer said, "Men, this might be the last formation you'll ever stand." For Milo it was, at least as an enlisted man.

He boarded a train headed to Chicago and took a window seat. He was fascinated as they rode along, and train after train came into view. It seemed they passed another huge array of coaches every ten minutes, virtually all of them taking military people back to their homes. When he arrived in Chicago, he transferred to an interurban train which stopped at Highwood, right next to Fort Sheridan. He checked into the Separation Center there and began the process of mustering out of the Army.

It took several days to get everything done. Among other things, he was counseled about his transition into civilian life and future employment. Job advice seemed to depend on your MOS—your Military Occupational Specialty number. Everyone in the military had one. If you were an infantry rifleman, your MOS was 745. Milo met with a VA job counselor who looked up his MOS in his manual and said, "745—you're qualified to be a walrus hunter." Milo thought that was pretty hilarious. He supposed he might have been told he was suited to be a truck driver, or a clerk, perhaps, but a walrus hunter?[2]

The Center fitted him out with two new, complete uniforms, and sewed his ribbons on the blouses. Ribbons stood for the awards a soldier had received so he didn't have to wear the actual medals. Milo hadn't worn a dress uniform for months. He tried on the new clothes, found he had a chest full of ribbons, and thought he looked pretty sharp. When his discharge was finally completed, he called his parents to say he was done and would be taking the interurban train up to Milwaukee. They told him to stay there, they'd drive down and pick him up at the train station. He killed time at the Center, and then, as the hour drew near for his folks to arrive, walked over to the station. With his spanking new uniform and imposing array of decorations, he was more than a little impressed with himself. Still too early to meet his parents, he went to the Fred Harvey to have a beer.

Today there are oases on Interstate Highways, travel stops with chain restaurants, bathroom facilities, and gift shops. Interstate highways didn't exist in those days, but there were similar facilities. Two chains, Fred Harvey and Howard Johnson's, operated oasis-like restaurants near major highways and train depots. Milo went into the bar and found he was its only customer. The bartender looked at him and said, "Where's your ID, sonny?" Milo couldn't produce one that said he was 21, and the man refused to serve him. It was very embarrassing: Staff Sergeant Milo Flaten, a seasoned combat veteran and highly decorated war hero, was four months shy of his twenty-first birthday. Not only did the bartender deny him alcohol, but wouldn't even let him stay on the premises. It was a huge blow to his ego, and Milo was understandably irritated.

His parents soon arrived in their 1937 Plymouth, and one can only imagine their joy at the reunion. They hadn't seen their son in two-and-a-half years. They knew he'd fought in some of the worst battles in the war and been seriously injured several times. For a month they had believed he was dead. After talking and reconnecting for a while, the family drove north on Highway 41 to Milwaukee and the Flaten apartment on Park Place and Murray. It was January 16, 1946, and Milo was home at last.

Chapter 15

The Home Front

Milo planned to go to college at the University of Wisconsin in Madison and play baseball. But when he got back home, the University was holding classes year-round on a three-semester basis. It was in the middle of a term, and he couldn't enroll until it ended. He decided to start at Wisconsin State Teachers College-Milwaukee (known by locals as Milwaukee State Teachers College)[1]. It was just about to begin a new spring semester, and Milo had barely enough time to sign up before classes started. He needed to carry twelve credits to qualify for GI Bill benefits, which amounted to payment of his tuition, books, and $50 per month cash. [2]

He got a job right away, playing string bass weekend nights on the Milwaukee Clipper, a 361-foot auto and passenger ferry which made regular trips across Lake Michigan between Milwaukee and Muskegon, Michigan. The ship could carry 900 passengers and 120 cars and was a popular vacation attraction. It had a nightclub with a dance floor and live band, staterooms, a movie theater, and several restaurants. It also provided an alternative way for motorists to travel between Wisconsin and Michigan without having to go through the busy Chicago corridor.

Between his studies and his job, Milo had little time for a social life. He rarely saw any of his old high school friends. When he did socialize, the people he hung out with were usually other vets. One of his haunts was a hotel bar near the Marquette University campus, a favorite of older Marquette students. He met and became friends with one of them, a guy named Mark Wheeler who played on the Marquette football team. He was dating a girl named George Ann Donald—George, as everyone called her—who came from Ashland, Wisconsin, and was a freshman at Milwaukee-Downer College. On one occasion Mark set Milo up with a blind date and the two couples attended a Downer dance together. The meeting didn't seem to touch off any particular interest between Milo and George.

That May, Milo got a summer job at Globe Union, the company his mother had worked for during the war. The firm made roller skates, car batteries, and spark plugs. He was a messenger on roller skates, delivering work orders, messages, and the like throughout the plant. Toward the end of summer, he left his job and moved to Madison to attend UW. He needed to get there early as the school had a fall baseball program, with practices starting before classes began. The baseball coach wanted him on the UW team, but couldn't provide a scholarship. He did offer a place to stay for free until the semester started, a dorm room located beneath the grandstand at Camp Randall, the school's football stadium. Milo took the offer and signed up for the baseball program.

He enrolled in the university as a political science major, with the idea that he would eventually go to the UW Law School. At the time the law school required three years of college credits for admission, and he had only one semester under his belt from the State Teacher's College. That was a future concern, but he had a more immediate issue to address: where to live once the semester started. With so many veterans taking advantage of the GI Bill, rooms were at a premium. He planned to go out for football as well as baseball. He'd grown since he joined the Army and felt he was big enough to play college ball (he wound up being 6' 2" and 238 pounds). He met some of the football team, including two players who had joined Delta Tau Delta, one of the school's Greek fraternities. They suggested he join too, as the house had sleeping rooms available. He pledged the fraternity and moved into the Delt house, a spacious building on the shore of Lake Mendota. ("Delt" was the usual nickname for the fraternity and its members.) It had a large living room, dining room, and kitchen on the first floor, and sleeping rooms on the second and third. Milo shared a room with four other students.

Money was always an issue for Milo; he was usually short of funds. Because his hearing had been badly impaired by his war injuries, he was eligible to receive $75 per month as a Disabled Veteran. Despite his constant need for cash, he never applied for the benefit. He considered being called disabled, even partially disabled, to be demeaning and embarrassing—much as he considered prisoner-of-war status. But he soon found out he could receive thirty-five dollars a month by joining the Army's Reserve Officer Training Corps (ROTC). That was considerably more appealing to him.

At UW, as at many other colleges, male students who were not veterans had to take either Army or Navy ROTC Basic Corps during their freshman and sophomore years. Basic cadets attended several classes a week in various military studies and had to spend one day a week in uniform. On that day, besides attending regular college classes, they participated in an hour-long formation in which they marched and learned close order drill. Basic cadets received college credit for their efforts, but no pay.

After the first two years of training, students could opt to quit or continue in ROTC. If they elected to stay on and were accepted by their branch, they signed up for the Advanced Corps. They would continue to attend military classes and formations for another two years, and at graduation would be commissioned as officers. But this second phase of training carried with it a serious obligation. An Advanced Corps student committed himself to serving a total of eight years in the military after being commissioned. Non-veterans had to serve a minimum of three years on active duty right after graduation. The balance could be served in the Regular Army or part-time in the Army Reserve or National Guard. Advanced Corps students received both college credit and pay as noted. Basic Corps training was waived for veterans like Milo, so he needed to spend only two years in Advanced Corps to become an officer. He signed up and passed the physical, somehow getting through the hearing test. He joined the Army Infantry program because it had been his branch during the war, and he felt comfortable with it.

Milo was an unusual veteran. Almost all the ex-GIs who went to UW after their discharge were extremely disdainful of ROTC. Milo was the only veteran in the UW Advanced ROTC Corps, and the program itself wasn't popular: there were only eight men in his class. Former enlisted men on campus made great fun of it and the students in it, especially on days when the cadets wore their uniforms. They ridiculed formations the students marched in and razzed any participants who were former GIs. Despite the poor reputation ROTC had with ex-GIs, Milo was very impressed with the education he received in his Military Science and Tactics course. It was intense training—more concentrated, he discovered, than cadets received at West Point. He liked that, and actually enjoyed some aspects of marching, too. With all his Army experience, it's not surprising he impressed his superiors. They admired the way he gave orders with authority and appointed him Adjutant, the cadet officer responsible for administration, personnel management, and record-keeping in his battalion.

In the spring of 1947, Milo met a couple of prelaw students who lived at the Batch, a four-story apartment building only a few blocks off campus. It was a roomier setting and a quieter atmosphere than the busy fraternity house, and he moved in with his new friends.

That summer he stayed with his parents at the farm they had purchased near River Falls, Wisconsin, and worked for the US Census Bureau. On Sunday afternoons he played baseball with the River Falls Falcons. He also spent six weeks attending the ROTC summer camp required of all advanced cadets. In fall, he returned to Madison and joined the UW football program. Milo had played center in high school and won the same position on the UW JV (junior varsity) team. He became the long snapper, the center for punts, field goals, and extra points. His father had trained him well, and with his strong arm, he was good at it. Other than that, he didn't consider himself much of a football player, although he did get into a couple of games that year. He thought his friendship with Earl "Jug" Girard, one of the team's stars, might have been what kept him on the roster.[3]

He returned to school in September of 1947, and for the next three semesters kept after his studies, his ROTC activities, and a part-time job here and there to pick up extra change. He also made an application to the University of Wisconsin Law School for attendance beginning in 1949. It was accepted.

After the close of the 1948 fall semester, three major events occurred in Milo's life. First, he completed his ROTC training, and on January 18, 1949, took part in the university's commencement ceremony—even though he wasn't graduating—to receive his Army Commission as a second lieutenant. He was pleased with his new status as an officer, but no longer had the thirty-five dollars he'd received each month from ROTC. He worried aloud about losing that income, and a friend suggested he join the local Army Reserve unit. As a 2nd lieutenant, he'd be paid fourteen dollars for each weekly meeting he attended, which was more each month than he'd been getting from ROTC. Milo joined the unit: Headquarters Company, Third Battalion, 334th Parachute Infantry Regiment, 84th Airborne Division. Other officers in the company were older guys, he said, around 28 to 30, and several were law school professors. The company now had only about a dozen enlisted men, a lot fewer than in prior years. All the officers were WWII veterans. The enlisted men were not—most had joined up to avoid the draft.

Milo was appointed the company's Executive Officer, or XO. As second in command, he ran the unit's day-to-day operations. The 334th Regiment had a heroic history during WWII, fighting in the Battle of the Bulge and other well-known campaigns. But now, in peacetime, it was more than casual—or, at least Milo's company was. Nobody bothered with uniforms or most military formalities. At weekly meetings the officers sat around and told stories about what they'd done and where they'd been during the war. It was like a private social club for veterans. Milo had only to show up and sign the attendance sheet to get paid. The "Armory" where they met was the second floor of a factory a few blocks from Camp Randall Stadium. It was nothing fancy, with chicken-wire cages holding equipment such as binoculars, blankets, and bayonets. But easygoing as it may have been, Milo's new company was an airborne unit. Its members were paratroopers, and if Milo wanted to continue his membership, he'd have to qualify for that specialty.

The second of Milo's important life events that year occurred in the early spring when he was spotted by a former Chicago White Sox scout who was impressed by his pitching skills. By the end of the semester, Milo had signed a contract with the White Sox organization and turned pro. Like all newcomers, he had to start at the bottom, in the minor leagues. The Northern League season began in mid-June, and he was sent to the Aberdeen, South Dakota, Jackrabbits (later renamed the Pheasants). When not on the road, the team lived in an old hotel Milo called a cheap, cheap dump. There weren't any bathrooms in the rooms or in the hotel itself. Players kept night jugs under their beds or went downstairs to the tavern below to use its facilities. It was a disagreeable way to live, but Milo's pitching quickly won seven games, and his manager said he would likely be promoted to a league with higher standing. He hoped a promotion would lead to better living conditions, but first, he had to report to his Army Reserve summer camp at Fort Riley, Kansas. Most of his experiences there pleased him, including the most intense training in Military Science and Tactics he'd ever had. However, it was Kansas, and it was a long, hot summer.

Having turned pro, Milo could no longer play college baseball when he returned to school that fall. In prior years, he wouldn't have been eligible to play any other college sport, either, but the rules had been changed, and he was still eligible for football.

The third landmark incident of the year, and the one that would have the longest-lasting influence on his life, occurred in late spring. While he had been living in Milwaukee he had a steady girlfriend, but after moving to Madison it became much more difficult for them to get together. Eventually both tired of traveling to meet and drifted apart, leaving Milo without female companionship.

Occasionally, Mark Wheeler would come over to Madison to see his girlfriend, George, who had just transferred to the UW. Wheeler always sought a free place to stay overnight, and Milo let him bunk in with him and his roommates. One weekend that spring the Delts partnered with Gamma Phi Beta sorority to have a beer party and supper at an area called Picnic Point, a park-like peninsula that juts out into Lake Mendota. It was a favorite spot for picnics, as the name implied, but also for beer parties and romantic meetings (eighteen-year-olds could legally drink beer in Wisconsin at that time.) George had joined Gamma Phi sorority after arriving at UW and was at the affair. Milo bumped into her, and this time sparks flew between them. They spent the rest of the day and as much of the evening as they could together. When Milo got back to his room, he called Mark Wheeler and told him to forget about coming over for more dates. He and George were now a couple. A serious couple.

During spring break in April 1949 Milo attended the two-week jump school at Fort Benning, Georgia. To earn his paratrooper's wings, he had to make seven jumps. After the initial preparatory training, he jumped from 5,000 feet, 2,000 feet, 1500 feet, and 900 feet, and did several night jumps. He was scared the first time he bailed out, but after that was no longer nervous. He liked the school; instructors treated trainees as officers and gentlemen. It was frigid in Georgia that spring, and to Milo it felt like winter. But other than being cold, he enjoyed the experience.

That summer Milo attended his first Army Reserve summer camp at Fort McCoy in Wisconsin. If discipline at the Headquarters Company's weekly meetings was lax, it was essentially non-existent during the two-week camp session. Located between the cities of Sparta and Tomah in western Wisconsin, the Fort had been an infantry training facility since it opened in 1909. It was located about twenty miles from Volk Field Air Force Base, where paratroopers could practice their jumps. However, it still had old, unheated wooden barracks and was usable only in summer months. Reveille was called so early in the morning that when the men turned out of their barracks, they were literally in the dark. Since no one could see them, they didn't bother to dress and wore only their underwear. Usually only five or six guys would show up, and they'd answer the roll call for everyone in the outfit. Nobody seemed to notice or care, probably a result of the casualness and close friendships they shared. Milo knew most of the officers in his unit from ROTC and the University. He believed he was one of their favorites, and could "get away with murder," as he put it.

The laxity at summer camps and reserve meetings lasted until a little after June 25, 1950, the day North Korea invaded South Korea. Thereafter, things became serious. Officers who didn't own uniforms went out and bought them. Rifles were issued, and other weapons and armaments appeared. Formal military protocol was followed; the days of sitting around and gabbing were over.

There was about to be another change, too; this one in Milo's domestic status. George was about to graduate, and Milo would have to stay in Madison for a couple more years to finish law school. He was afraid if George returned home, she'd find someone else, and he'd lose her. He asked her to marry him and she said yes. They made plans for a wedding at her home in Ashland the next January, during Christmas vacation.

Chapter 16

Déjà Vu

George and Milo were married in Ashland on January 28, 1950, and after a brief honeymoon set up housekeeping in Madison. Milo returned to his classes, while George went to work for the UW Extension Department, organizing summer music clinics for bands, choirs, and orchestras throughout the state.

When summer came, Milo was upgraded to a higher-ranking baseball team in the White Sox organization, the Columbus, Georgia, Cardinals in the AA South Atlantic League. He was disappointed to find his teammates were, in his estimation, dumb southerners with whom he had nothing in common. It was much like when he joined the Army: he made few friends and again felt isolated. Yet his pitching was good enough to win another promotion, this time to the Denver Bears in the Pacific Coast League. Unfortunately, he didn't fare as well there. Far too many of his pitches were hit out of the park. He thought it was probably the thin air at the city's mile-high altitude, but whatever the cause, saw little hope for himself as a pro. No doubt he also missed his new bride and married life. Whatever his motivation, he quit the team and returned to Madison where he enrolled in summer school.

Milo and George's Wedding, January 28, 1950

Early in the summer of 1951, the Flatens received dismaying news: Milo was being called to active Army duty. It was not his whole reserve unit being called up, but only a few officers needed as replacements. It was pretty clear Milo was headed for a combat zone again. The Korean War had been ongoing for a year. What had started as a border war between North and South Korea escalated when China entered the conflict as North Korea's ally and sent hordes of soldiers to the region. Many Americans perceived the conflict as what might be the first of possible communist attacks upon democratic nations. The US, already there to support South Korea, reacted by sending more of its soldiers to help. Milo knew he was subject to being summoned to active duty at any time, but the call-up must have been devastating news, particularly for

George. Milo was used to Army ways from his prior service, but that was before he met George, and it was all new to her.

Milo flew to Seoul, South Korea, and from there was trucked to his duty station, a mountain which he would come to call Pork Chop Hill.[1] He was attached to a rifle company in the Third Infantry Division, a front-line position. The garrison was about halfway down the mountain, with another US installation at the top. Milo's post was a bunker reinforced by logs and sand, with firing holes through which the GIs could shoot. Rooms and beds of a sort were dug into the hill, so there was greater protection than a foxhole would offer. If one walked around openly on the hill, he'd likely draw fire. But other than that, it was the GIs here and the Chinese over there, and it seemed to Milo no one was making rash attacks to change things.

His company hadn't lost a lot of men and didn't need any replacements; they were being sent in without regard to whether there were slots needing to be filled. As a result, Milo's new CO didn't know what to do with him. After a couple of days, he was assigned to train enlisted men in calisthenics, map reading, and telephone communications. Nobody in his new unit knew about his extensive combat experience in WWII, and he wasn't about to volunteer it. In his opinion, officers did their best keeping their mouths shut about such things.

Thirteen days after his arrival, Milo finally received orders to do something besides training. He was ordered to lead a night recon patrol to a stream at the foot of the mountain. The soldiers were to set up a listening post and report anything they observed or heard. Milo picked five enlisted men to go with him. Two of them had been on earlier missions to the same area and found their way to it in the dark. Seconds after arriving they heard loud noises: shouting, guns firing, bugles being blown, and the crashing of cymbals. One of the soldiers said, "I think they're coming, Lieutenant." Milo phoned HQ and ordered flares. They were shot from mortars and held aloft for a time by parachutes. When the second flare lit the area, the men saw a large group of Chinese forces attacking toward their position. Milo didn't know what was happening, but GIs who had been stationed there a while recognized the situation. Once a month or so the Chinese officers would give their troops liquor and drugs. The men would get in violent, crazy moods and make reckless, almost suicidal attacks on the Americans and ROKs (Republic of South Korea soldiers). Milo called for mortar fire and then gave what he would later say was the most important order of his military career: "Haul ass!"

The patrol turned and started to run back toward their post when history bizarrely repeated itself. A piece of shrapnel from an enemy mortar struck Milo, and he collapsed to the ground, unconscious. The shard blew through his helmet and liner and lodged in his skull at the top of his head, only an inch from the fragment he'd carried since 1944. His men rushed to carry him back to their lines, and from there he was evacuated to the States. He woke up at Letterman Army Hospital at the Presidio in San Francisco. As before, doctors decided not to operate and left the piece of metal in place.[2] Its presence didn't seem to interfere with healing or with any physical or mental ability, and Milo's convalescence progressed quickly. After a month he was doing quite well and walking around outside as often as he could.

The Army's policy was to move recovering wounded personnel to Army hospitals as close to their homes as possible. It transferred Milo to Percy Jones General Hospital in Battle Creek, Michigan. He was there a week, and each day he became more frustrated and concerned about his future. What could be his last semester of law school at UW would start soon, and he didn't want to miss it. He felt fully recovered, and no one had told him otherwise, so he decided to go home. He called the railroad depot and bought a ticket to Madison. He went to the hospital's main desk, and told the officer of the day he was leaving and going home. Although he had no orders, nobody argued with him or called MPs. He rode a cab to the station and boarded his train.

In Madison, though, he realized he had a problem. Normally he'd have reported to his old company in the 334th Regiment. But while he was gone that regiment and the entire 84th Division had been transferred to Milwaukee. A different reserve unit, the 441st

Battle Group, 103rd Division, had been assigned to Madison. A Battle Group was a post-WWII formation usually based on an existing battalion, with the addition of artillery, armor, and other units. There was no one from his unit to report to, and he didn't have orders assigning him elsewhere. It took the CO of the 441st several days to get the mess untangled, but finally Milo was discharged from active duty and transferred into the local reserve unit.

It had been a harrowing time for George, not knowing how badly Milo had been injured or what his condition would be when he got home. The two gratefully resumed their life together. She continued working for the University. Milo made it back early enough to register for the fall semester, and went back to his law school classes. He also stayed active in the Army Reserve, attending weekly and monthly drills. At last, on February 13, 1952, he graduated from law school and received his LLB degree;[3] he was now Milo G. Flaten, Jr., Attorney at Law.

Epilogue

fter serving a required six-month apprenticeship with a Madison law firm, Milo was offered a full-time job with the same firm and began his career as a trial lawyer.[1] In the ensuing years, he would have a successful law practice and serve several terms as an Alderman on the Madison City Council. He and George raised two sons, Mike and Dan, and a daughter, Cathy.

In the Reserve he actively sought promotions, and continued to advance in his military career. But even though he maintained his status as a paratrooper and served another 31 years in the Army Reserve after Korea, he never faced combat again. He badly wanted to be a general and did all he could think of to get promoted. Unfortunately, army regulations prevailed, and forced him to retire in 1982 as a colonel.

In 1986 his beloved wife, George, died of cancer at the age of 59. It was a devastating time for Milo. George remained at home during her illness and Milo stayed with her and became her caregiver. He referred all his clients to other lawyers, and although he kept paying rent and expenses for his office, almost never went there. When George passed, he had no money, no clients, and no cases. His luck held again; with the assistance of friends, he became a free-lance arbitrator, and soon enjoyed a successful career in that field. He didn't retire from hearing cases until failing health required it. His last opinion was published only a few months before his death. It involved the Sauk County, Wisconsin, Deputy Sheriff's organization claim for higher wages. While many of his cases involved Wisconsin parties, like this one, he heard major cases as well in distant venues, often involving huge nationwide companies and organizations. These cases were not assigned to him. The battling parties themselves had to seek him out and agree specifically that he be hired to resolve their issues. It was clear evidence of how well known and respected he was.

Milo in his middle years in Madison

In August of 2009, Milo took part in a Freedom Flight to Washington, D.C., to visit the World War II Memorial. All the veterans who went were treated royally. Milo thoroughly enjoyed the experience, but it was the return to Wisconsin which pleased him most. His son, Dan, and Dan's family met him as he got off the plane in

Milwaukee. The terminal was crowded, and as the old soldiers emerged from the ramp, other passengers in the concourse recognized the men as WWII vets. They stood and clapped, celebrating them as heroes. Milo was taken by surprise. WWII veterans had been shown appreciation when they returned from their war and didn't get the cold reception Vietnam vets received when they came home. Still, to have people honoring him and his comrades for their service almost 65 years earlier was a very moving experience for Milo. He was uncharacteristically emotional when he talked about it.

Milo, at age 84 in Madison, Fall of 2009

In mid-December 2012, Milo was diagnosed with congenital heart failure. He moved into a succession of assisted living residences and had difficulty adapting to that kind of living arrangement. Finally, his family found a facility that pleased both them and Milo. But his disease progressed, and he grew weaker with each day. Finally, one Saturday in March he stopped getting out of bed.

The next morning he announced he didn't want to talk to anyone. However, later that afternoon he changed his mind, got into a wheelchair, and his family wheeled him down to the nurse's station. In a last burst of energy, he sat there for several hours, telling the nursing staff about Omaha Beach and the war and all the rest. When he finally tired and returned to bed, his son Mike and daughter Cathy's husband Steve stayed with him. They talked of old times and told more stories on into the night until Milo eventually closed his eyes and took a final breath. It was by then Monday morning, March 11, 2013. Milo had lived to be 87 years and 10 months. His funeral was held on March 15th, his body was cremated, and his ashes were interred next to George's. The valiant warrior was gone, and all that was left were memories.

End of story, as Milo often said.

Afterword

There is certainly more that should be said about Milo. His life was full of interesting stories: tales of funny, amazing, even outrageous antics. What fascinated me most, though, was learning the experiences of a man who lived through some of the worst battles of World War II, historical events most of us have only read about. It's amazing to me he didn't perish on D-Day. That he lived and continued fighting until the war in Europe was over, is truly mind-boggling. I know others had similar experiences and also survived, but the odds they faced and the hardships they endured were so daunting I don't understand how any of them could have done it.

Like his cohorts who served in that horrible war, Milo is considered a hero by those of us who weren't there—perhaps by many who were there, too. I never asked him if he thought he was a hero. I've read about other soldiers who've come back from a war and insisted they were not heroic. They believed the men who died or were permanently injured earned that status. I can understand why they might feel that way. They well knew that much of what takes place in combat occurs haphazardly. In the chaos and craziness, who can predict who will live and who will die? Which bullet will find its mark and which will drop to the ground? Which shell will detonate and which will bury itself in the dirt, unexploded? There's no formula or equation that allows one to figure that out. Milo was clear—he didn't know how he made it. There were days he was sure he was going to die, and yet he didn't. Unquestionably, he was absurdly lucky. But I believe more than just luck was at work. Milo didn't say much about his skills or the tactics he employed, but he did say he kept his head down. That's an important point. He was a smart young man who used his good sense whenever possible to protect himself, even while performing acts of valor and bravery. He was in dangerous conditions almost all the time, but kept his wits about him and did whatever he could to lessen the peril. Those wits, that native intelligence, clearly continued to shine brightly throughout the rest of his life.

He was also a natural-born leader. On his first day in combat as a buck private he took over a faltering company-sized group of young men and led them into battle. His abilities were soon recognized, and he rose from private to tech sergeant within a few months. He was recognized for his actions and given numerous medals: a Silver Star, two Bronze Stars for valor, and seven Purple Hearts (although he probably was injured more than fifteen times). Those military leadership qualities were in evidence in later years, as he attained higher ranks and positions in the Army Reserve.

It must also be said he was an efficient killer, part of a deadly war machine. We don't talk much about the taking of lives that happens during wars. Most combat veterans don't seem to want to, especially with those who've never been in battle. For most of the rest of us, it's a horrific subject. What mother, for instance, wants to hear her twenty-year-old son talk about the human beings he shot or blew up, or killed with his bayonet or his hands? Yet it must be acknowledged: any infantryman who lived through that war became very adept at slaughter. As Milo realized, it was kill or be killed. I have no idea how many lives Milo took. I never asked, and he never volunteered. He probably had no idea himself, and wouldn't have wanted to know. The fact is, though, there had to have been many; he was in the middle of some of the bloodiest battles of World War

II. He was a skilled combatant whose rise in the ranks can be attributed not only to his leadership abilities but to his expertise in bloodshed and destruction.

Lastly, what about what is perhaps the most dramatic aspect of his life: that he might have been the first American infantry invader to land on Omaha Beach? It's doubtful anyone knows who was first on the beach. Nobody was assigned to watch for such things or keep notes. Who knows if anyone was even thinking then that arriving first was a notable feat or something exceptional? Anyone there was simply trying to stay alive.

I would venture to say there is no question Milo was the first GI to reach the beach in the sector where he landed. But Omaha Beach was miles long, and in the rain and mist, Milo wouldn't have even been able to see troops landing in distant areas. Many of the landing craft in the first wave, and especially Milo's, were carried far beyond their intended landing zone by wind and current, thus adding considerable time to their journey and distance from each other.

But does it really matter who was first? Whether Milo was or not, I remain fascinated he was there at H-Hour on the historic event we call D-Day. Yet, it must be noted, his presence was as much a matter of chance as anything else. He was not responsible for placing himself in that place at that moment, nor does he merit commendation for it. Recognition for "who got there first" may be appropriate for the record books, but it means little in these circumstances. In my opinion *all* the men who took part in the invasion were heroes. The fact that Milo was one of the first who braved the landing on Omaha Beach says enough. That, and that against all odds he went on to fight for months in some of the worst imaginable combat in the war. And, further, that he returned home, almost whole, to live another 67 productive, successful years. In my book, that's nothing short of heroic.

Acknowledgments

I owe many for their assistance, their great suggestions, and their moral support. I am indebted to Milo Flaten's three children, Cathy Flaten-Jones, Daniel Flaten, and Michael Flaten, for encouraging my efforts and providing information about their father.

David Ranney and David Westring read early versions and independently gave essentially the same advice, which was not only sound but critical. Unfortunately, it took me several years to realize how important their ideas were, and to make revisions based on them. Richard Purinton not only offered manuscript suggestions, but gave me helpful guidance regarding the publication process. Others who read early versions and offered wise counsel include Donna Briesemeister, Charles Grandy, Laura Hale, Sam White and Bruce Nason. My sincere thanks to you all.

I'm also greatly thankful to Alex McDonald, who created the informative maps and charts included in the book, and who advised me on a number of matters, including computer issues and procedures far beyond an old Luddite's comprehension. I can't give enough thanks to my old friend, Jim Gerard, for photo editing, and I am beholden to Peter and Caroline O'Connor and their company, Bespoke Book Covers, who have become new friends. They have been so gracious in providing their services and the careful handholding I came to realize I needed badly.

Finally, I am immensely grateful for all that my editor, Barbara Greenfeldt, has contributed to this endeavor, lending her considerable talents to almost every aspect of the project. Working with her has been a privilege and a great pleasure.

Notes

Introduction

1. Forrest Gump is the principal fictional character in a movie entitled *Forrest Gump* which opened in theaters in 1994 and won the Oscar for Best Picture in 1995. It starred Tom Hanks as Forrest, a young man with a low IQ who excels at many things, including running. He is a heroic soldier in the Viet Nam war, and constantly runs into famous people (Elvis Presley for one) and historic events without trying. The movie was based on a book, also called *Forrest Gump*, written by Winston Groom and published in 1986.

2. A request was made for Milo's military service records, but the Department of Veterans Affairs advised they had been destroyed in a warehouse fire in the 1980s.

Chapter One

1. When the United States entered the War in 1941 the Army consisted of the Regular Army (full-time soldiers), the Army Reserve, and the Army National Guard (both of the latter being part-time units with citizen soldiers). The Army of the United States

(AUS) was created as an entity to contain all of the soldiers and units in the above organizations, as well as those civilians who were conscripted (drafted) or volunteered. At the end of the war the AUS was deactivated, and all Army personnel returned to the outfits they had belonged to before the war—or were permanently discharged if they had volunteered or been drafted.

2. Originally called leggings, they were pieces of heavy canvas strapped on the leg from mid-shoe to just under the knee, to protect the lower leg. Milo insisted upon calling them "leggins."

Chapter Two

1. Kathy (originally named Cathy until the Army changed it) was a beautiful young woman who started a modeling career while still in high school. After graduation she moved to New York to attend a prestigious acting school. However, after the war started, she enlisted in the WACs (Women's Army Corps) and wound up stationed in Florida. There she met and began seeing a handsome young Army officer, Roscoe Karns, Jr.; his friends all called him Rocky. His father, Roscoe Karns, Sr., had become quite famous as a result of a long career in vaudeville and the movies. Rocky and Kathy were married, moved to Hollywood after the war, and began auditioning for film roles. Kathy was in a couple of movies but didn't stay long in the business. Rocky established something of a career, however. In 1946, he played the war hero brother of George Bailey (Jimmy Stewart) in Frank Capra's classic film, *It's A Wonderful Life*. Unfortunately, most of his subsequent roles were minor and didn't pay enough to support the young family. In the mid-fifties, Rocky left show business to work in the sales field, and they moved to New York State. In 1971, Rocky, Kathy, and their three children moved to Ajijic, Mexico, a beautiful lakeside resort town about 35 miles south of Guadalajara. Kathy ran an acting school and Rocky operated the couple's English-speaking theater. In addition to acting, producing, and directing, Rocky took up painting and became an accomplished artist. He passed away in 2000, and Milo greatly grieved the loss. He and his brother-in-law had become

close friends. Incidentally, Kathy wasn't alone in having the military change her name. Some WWII Army records show Milo's name as Malo Flaton.

2. Andy, Robert G. Anders, would see combat during WWII, graduate from the Foreign Service School at Georgetown University in Washington, D.C., and begin a diplomatic career with the State Department. After postings in Rangoon, Burma (now Myanmar) and Manila he was working as a Consular Officer in the American Embassy in Iran when it was taken over by Iranians in 1979. He was one of the six Americans who escaped and were hidden at the Canadian Ambassador's home. Eventually, the six were taken out of Iran by a CIA ruse involving a fake film crew. That story has now been well told in the 2012 prize-winning movie *Argo*. Anders was portrayed in the film by the actor Tate Donovan.

Chapter Three

1. That battle was one of the Allies' most disastrous failures in World War II. It was handled so badly it became the subject of a Congressional inquiry after the war.

2. Neither Queen's life as a luxury liner would begin until after the war.

Chapter Four

1. Company A, for instance, came from Bedford, VA, a town that would become famous for losing the largest percentage of its population on D-Day.

2. The author searched for evidence of a Robert Hirsch (and other spellings of the name Milo gave only orally) but was unable to find any. It is likely simply an error in Milo's memory; as noted, he also called his company commander by the wrong name. (See note 1, Chapter Seven.)

3. The WWII landing craft most often referred to today is the LST, (Landing Ship, Tank) a large vessel designed to carry men,

tanks, and tracked vehicles. It measured over 300 feet in length, had a fifty-foot beam, and a crew of over a hundred.

4. Milo's was not the only bare head that embarked for the Normandy invasion. Quite a number of GIs shaved their heads as a sign of their warrior status. Others wore Mohawk haircuts, presumably hoping to look fierce to the enemy in their coming battles.

Chapter Six

1. GIs also called Germans nicknames such as Dutch, Fritz, Herman, and Jerry (as "Jerry is just over that ridge"). Hun, Heinie, and Bosch were also used as demeaning terms. Milo's favorite seemed to be "kraut," and he fully intended it to be disparaging. He and his fellow soldiers loathed their enemy, and didn't hesitate to defame them—as well as kill them.

2. It was the first and last time Milo would wear a gas mask; Germany never did use poisonous gas in WWII.

Chapter Seven

1. Milo told me his company commander was a Captain Steward who was from New Mexico, and had survived D-Day for many weeks, at the least. It is documented that throughout Milo's training in England the CO of E Company of the 116th was Capt. Laurence Madill. Capt. Madill was fatally wounded in the first wave on Omaha Beach as he went back to get more ammunition for his men. There is evidence 1st Lt. Robert Garcia, the company's XO, was promoted to captain and succeeded Madill as CO. Records indicate he commanded E Company at least until the end of July, when he was reported as being wounded. I thought Milo's identification with the man he remembered was so strong I shouldn't change it.

2. His assumptions at the time proved to be correct. In all the years that followed, he would never hear of any additional survivors, and would never get an invitation to a reunion.

3. Weeks later, he thought he recognized another man from his boat, but he wasn't sure, and he never learned if he was right.

4. Remarkably, once the war ended, he quit smoking and never started again.

5. The author believes he discovered one of the town's famous sons. In olden France, residents often took their last name from the place they called home, usually starting it with a "de'," or "d"—as Charles de Gaulle's ancestors apparently did. Many of those old last names were kept by descendants, as in the case of Walt Disney's family.

6. During the German occupation of France, many French citizens joined the resistance movement. They were called the Free French Forces, and by 1944 numbered over 400,000. Many took part in the Normandy invasion. After portions of France were liberated, resistance fighters were organized into more traditional army units designated by General de Gaulle as FFI, or "French Forces of the Interior." When France was fully freed the FFI was disbanded, and its troops were incorporated into the Regular French Army.

6. General De Gaulle led France after the war as head of the Provisional Government of the French Republic (1944-1946), as Prime Minister (1958-1959), and as President (1959-1969).

Chapter Eight

1. "SS" stood for Schutzstaffel, meaning protective squadron. The organization began as Hitler's personal bodyguard in the 1920's, but eventually became a huge Nazi paramilitary unit. SS units fought in WWII alongside regular German Army troops and were noted for being fierce combatants. Germans considered them the elite ranks of the German military. However, SS units conducted many of the horrible atrocities and crimes against humanity committed by the Nazis. The SS was banned as a criminal organization after the war ended, and many of its members were prosecuted.

2. Needlessly killed and wounded, Milo thought. He was quite angry about it then and his ire would remain for the rest of his life. He felt Generals Eisenhower and Bradley should have been court-martialed for their failure to obtain adequate intelligence about the

Normandy countryside. Had planners known about the French hedgerows, the inherent problems could have been addressed.

Chapter Nine

1. After WWII Milo found a spot near his home that reminded him of Martinville and its adjacent hills and valley. The little town is also called Martinville and is located north of Madison, Wisconsin, near Cross Plains. Milo said a church there looks exactly like the churches he saw in Normandy. He stopped once to talk to its priest and was told the town and church were named by the first priest to serve there. He was French, and Milo assumed that he came from the French community of the same name. Milo said he visited the locale every so often in order to remember just how frightened he had been. The author traveled there with him one afternoon to see what it looked like. It was a beautiful, lush area. As we drove up the valley, he exclaimed about how much it looked like the French region. He pointed ahead to some hills and said, "The Germans were right up there, and we were down here going after them." His excitement was palpable.

2. Milo would meet Dinah Shore years later and tell her he'd been in the group of soldiers she entertained. She said she remembered the occasion very well.

Chapter Ten

1. Years later, Milo would say he'd done a lot of things more deserving in his months of combat, but that day he was seen by a CO. He said getting decorated was always a matter of luck in the infantry. A lot of heroism went unrecognized because there were no officers nearby to observe it. When Milo was in Holland his company commander was walking where he shouldn't have been, and got a bullet in his leg. Milo was nearby and dragged the officer to the aid station. The CO put Milo up for a Bronze Star, which Milo thought was rather ironic. He'd done the same thing a number of times for other guys and never even got a thank you.

2. His embarrassment continued for the rest of his life, and he could never tell his father what had happened. He would never understand why anyone would flaunt the fact that he had been captured and advertise it on his car license plates as a badge of honor. To him that was a terrible admission of failure.

Chapter Eleven

1. In fact, Springfield '03s were so accurate, snipers continued to use them in the Korean War and in the early years of Vietnam.

2. Milo would carry the piece of metal in his skull for the rest of his life. In his later years, it was easy to see on his bald pate.

Chapter Twelve

1. Desmond had gained substantial fame as a singer and would go on to a postwar career as a popular movie actor.

2. The name "gypsy" had been given to Reinhardt's people years ago. It was thought then that they were from Egypt because of their dark skin. Actually, they were called Roma, and had descended from a group that emigrated to Europe from central India in the 12th and 13th centuries. The Roma had a very insular culture and seemed quite foreign to other Europeans. Most lived as nomads, traveling together in horse-drawn wagons called caravans, the early equivalent of modern RVs.

3. Django became world-famous, and after the war traveled to the US on numerous occasions to give concerts and tour with Duke Ellington. He died at 43 from a brain hemorrhage. His music continues to be popular among jazz fans to this day. There are a significant number of well-received tribute bands playing Django's music today in the United States and abroad.

Chapter Thirteen

1. Milo found out later one of the people crossing the bridge had been Werner von Braun. Although he'd been a member of the Nazi

Party, von Braun and his colleagues were welcomed by the Americans, and would go on to become the architects and directors of the U.S. space program.

Chapter Fourteen

1. At one time the author worked with a man who had been a Nazi SS trooper. At age 16, close to the end of the war, he was promoted from Hitler's Youth Corps (somewhat similar to the Boy Scouts) to an SS infantry unit. On his first day of duty, he was ordered to take a position against advancing GIs to protect his outfit, which was desperately retreating. He hid behind a log, and before he was able to shoot his rifle was hit by American fire which injured his leg, and blinded him in one eye. He became an American citizen in his twenties, and forty years later was still excited to show me the document he had received when processed out of the German Army: his Denazification Papers. Typed in German on onion skin paper they had almost deteriorated. He was exceedingly proud of having them.

2. Some years later, Milo met a retired walrus hunter and told him about the counselor at the Separation Center. The man said, "You should have taken his advice. It's a good job." He said he had made over $100,000 a year and retired before he reached forty. Milo had to agree, it would have been a very lucrative job.

Chapter Fifteen

1. It would later become the University of Wisconsin-Milwaukee.

2. To those used to present day tuition charges, one might assume these were very generous benefits. In fact, they weren't that great. Milo didn't remember the amount of his tuition per semester, but some ten years later it was still only about $50.00 per semester (roughly $665.00 in today's money).

3. A native of Marinette, Wisconsin, Girard enrolled at UW in 1944 as a 17-year-old freshman. His first year was so successful he was named a first team All-American by Look magazine. Drafted

into the Army after his freshman season, Girard served in World War II, and returned to UW in 1947 to play one more season. Although he had attended Wisconsin for only two years, he was drafted in the first round by both the Green Bay Packers and the Cleveland Indians baseball team. After a brief stint in the Indians' farm system, he joined the Packers, and played from 1948-51. He was then traded, and played for the Detroit Lions, from 1952-56. He played one more year of pro football with the Pittsburgh Steelers before retiring in 1957. He was considered both a star and a noted character in American sports.

Chapter Sixteen

1. A Korean mountain called Pork Chop Hill became notorious after the Korean War, having received its name as a result of numerous bloody battles that took place there. Officially it was called Hill 255, an outpost in the mountains of the Korean Peninsula quite close to the 38th parallel, the border between North and South Korea. After hostilities ceased, it became part of the Demilitarized Zone (DMZ). By 1951 it had changed hands several times. Finally, in 1953, there was a huge battle for it which would be chronicled in a 1959 movie called *Pork Chop Hill*, starring Gregory Peck. The name was well-known thereafter.

Milo claimed the mountain he was on was on was called Pork Chop Hill. The author couldn't substantiate that Milo was actually on the mountain depicted in the 1959 movie, but it seems clear the name didn't become well known to the public until long after Milo left the area. My guess is that in later years he adopted the name for the mountain where he was stationed, whether intentionally or not. The author considers that to be of little importance. One could say all the mountains in Korea where US troops saw battle were Pork Chop Hills. The author allowed Milo's references to the famous mountain to stand.

2. Both pieces of shrapnel were easily seen in Milo's later years, after he lost all his hair.

3. LLB stood for Bachelor of Letters and Laws, the degree

conferred on law school graduates until the late 1960s. The degree was changed to Juris Doctor at that time by most law schools, given that recipients had spent three years in graduate school, and already possessed a bachelor's degree. The change was retroactive; all attorneys with LLB's could apply to change their degree to a JD, and almost all practicing lawyers did.

Epilogue

1. One of the first trials his firm assigned him to was notable, another of those instances when he came face-to-face with famous people of the time. It wasn't a big case but was still a daunting experience to the fledgling lawyer. The lawsuit had been brought before a Justice of the Peace in Dodgeville, Wisconsin (small claims courts had not yet been created in the state). The plaintiff was Milo's client, a local grocery store, and the defendant was the world-renowned architect Frank Lloyd Wright. The suit involved unpaid bills owed to the store. Milo was told that Wright was known locally for not paying his bills in a timely fashion. He was also an exceedingly dramatic personage and appeared in court that day wearing a cape and a white homburg hat. Following extensive pretrial discussion, the matter was eventually settled for something less than the full amount of the claim. While there was no dramatic trial or victory for Milo, the uniqueness of the experience would stay firmly in his memory.

Glossary

AEF
Allied Expeditionary Force: a name given to the Allied joint forces (British, Canadian, etc.) fighting in Europe in 1943 until the end of the war; it was commanded by General Eisenhower (SHAEF, Supreme Headquarters Allied Expeditionary Forces). See also ETO, European Theater of Operations.

Allies
The name adopted by the nations that banded together to wage war upon Germany, Italy and Japan, the nations known as The Axis (see Axis, below).

Ammo
Ammunition for weapons.

Armor
A thick coating of metal to protect structures and vehicles from bullets and shells; also, some armored vehicles themselves were called armor, such as tanks, personnel carriers, self-propelled artillery, and tank destroyers.

Army
The name of the American military branch consisting of land-based soldiers. In WWII, the US Army also contained the Air Force, which became a separate branch in 1947.
The term "Army" also designated a unit made up of two or more US Army Corps.

Army Group
A US Army formation containing two or more Armies (see Army, above).

ASTP
Army Specialized Training Program; a program designed to send soldiers to college while on active duty.

AUS
Army of the United States, the entity created during WWII to include members of the Regular Army, the Army Reserve, Army National Guard units, as well as draftees and volunteers. It was dissolved at the end of the war.

Axis
The name adopted by Germany, Italy and Japan who joined together to fight against the Allies during World War II (see Allies, above).

Bandolier
A web belt which held clips of ammunition for rifles.

Bangalore Torpedo
A device made of metal pipe containing explosives, used to blow openings in concertina or barbed wire barriers.

BAR
Browning Automatic Rifle; a machine gun that looks like a large rifle.

Barrage
A bombardment, or volley of shelling from canons. See also salvo, below.

Basic Training
The indoctrination and training given to new soldiers.

Battalion
US Army unit including three companies; also see BTN, below.

Battle Fatigue
Also called combat fatigue, combat exhaustion or shell shock: a psychiatric disorder brought on by the stress of war which causes soldiers to stop fighting and become essentially helpless.

Bazooka
A shoulder-held rocket launcher.

Beam
The width of a boat or ship.

Billet
A non-military location, such as a private home, used temporarily to house soldiers.

Bocage
A woodland area in which hedgerows (see below) are used to delineate pastures and keep herds of cattle intact.

Boot
A trainee attending "boot camp;" see below.

Boot Camp
A slang name for Basic Training.

Bosun
Short for Boatswain, a US Navy Warrant Officer in charge of the
Deck Department of a ship.

Bosun's whistle
A shrill whistling device used to get the attention of naval personnel. Also called a Boatswain's (or bosun's) pipe or call.

Brass
Slang name for officers in high positions or of high rank.

Brigade
The type of unit Gen. Jackson commanded in the Civil War, the
forerunner of the 116th Regiment in WWII.

BTN
See Battalion, above.

Buck private
Slang name of the lowest rank of private.

Buck sergeant
Slang name for the lowest rank of sergeant.

Bunker
A small fort used by Germany in WWII, usually partially buried,
made of rocks, concrete and steel, with openings allowing its
soldiers to fire on the Allies. See Pillbox, below.

Buzz Bombs
German V-1 and V-2 rockets, also called Flying Bombs and
Doodlebugs, used to bomb England during WWII.

CAS
See Close Air Support, below.

CG
Commanding General, the general officer in charge of a military unit, usually a regiment or larger.

Chevrons
The stripes on an enlisted man's sleeve indicating his rank.

Close Air Support
War planes assisting infantry soldiers by bombing and strafing the enemy. Abbreviated CAS.

CO
Commanding Officer, the officer in charge of any unit larger than a squad.

Combat Exhaustion
See Battle Fatigue.

Combat Fatigue
See Battle Fatigue, above.

Company
Abbreviated Co., an Army unit containing three platoons.

Concertina Wire
Rolls of razor-sharp barbed wire used by the Germans to deter invading forces.

Conscription
The process by which a government orders citizens into its military ranks. See Draft, below.

CP
Command Post; the headquarters of a US Army unit (regimental, division, corps, etc.).

CPO
Chief Petty Officer, a US Navy non-com equivalent to an Army
staff sergeant.

Corps
A US Army formation containing two or more divisions.

Coxswain
A US Navy enlisted man in charge of a small boat carried by a large
ship, such as a Higgins boat (LCVP).

Davit
A marine crane mounted on a ship, used to hold and launch smaller
crafts such as Higgins boats or lifeboats.

DIV
Division; a US Army unit containing three regiments.

Division
See DIV, above.

Dog Robber
An enlisted soldier serving as an officer's orderly or valet.

Draft
See Conscription, above.

Entrenching Tool
A shovel carried by GIs on their belt, used primarily for digging
foxholes. The blade portion folded back against the handle, making
it easier to transport.

ETO
European Theater of Operations United States Army (ETOUSA);
from 1942 through 1945; a group similar to but separate from
SHAEF in planning and executing warfare for the Allies in Europe.

European Theater of Operations
See ETO, above.

Final Protective Line
A line of soldiers firing machine guns or rifles into an area ahead of them to prevent enemy troops from moving closer and assaulting their position.

FO
Forward Observer: a member of the armed forces who is positioned near the front line and directs the firing of weapons from the infantry, artillery, naval vessels or aircraft.

Furlough
A temporary leave of absence from duty; see also Leave.

Garrison
A group of military personnel whose job is to protect their town or location.

GI
The name soldiers were often called in WWII. It apparently stemmed from a label at first on garbage cans in the early 1900's standing for galvanized iron. Later it was interpreted to have meant Government Issue and GI was stamped on many Army items and pieces of equipment. Some soldiers started using the term as a description for themselves, and the practice became popular and commonly used throughout the Army.

Gold
The code name of one of the D-Day beaches.

HE
Heavy Explosives: a type of shell used by the US Army or Navy in WWII.

Hedgehog
A steel structure planted on French beaches by the Germans to prevent tanks and other vehicles from invading.

Hedgerow
A berm or raised earthworks topped with spiny plants; used by farmers in England and France as fences to enclose their pastures and keep their herds of cattle intact.

Higgins Boat
A landing craft capable of transporting up to 36 soldiers from a troop ship to shore; its formal military designation was LCVP (Landing Craft, Vehicle, Personnel).

HQ
Headquarters.

INF
Infantry; foot soldiers.

Infantry
See INF, above.

Intel
Intelligence; data or information.

Jam Session, jam
Originally a jazz term describing a group of musicians playing together creating improvised arrangements of songs or chord progressions on the spot. To jam is to ad lib, or improvise.

Juno
The code name of one of the D-Day beaches.

KP
Kitchen Police: Army food service workers.

LCVP
Landing Craft, Vehicle, Personnel; see Higgins Boat, above.

LD
Line of Departure; a site where troops amass before an invasion or offensive maneuver so they may attack together as a coordinated effort.

Leave
See Furlough.

LST
Landing Ship Tank; a large ship used to bring tanks, other armor, and personnel to shore.

Leggins
Originally "leggings;" tough leather pieces strapped around the lower leg to protect the shin; later supplanted by combat boots.

Mae West
An inflatable life jacket named after the curvy Broadway and Hollywood actress of the '40s.

Mess
The military term for food service.

Moor
A tract of mostly empty, uncultivated land in England containing grass and low vegetation; used by Americans for training during WWII.

Motor March
See Shuttle March below.

MP
Army Military Police.

NCO
Non-Commissioned Officer; corporals and sergeants in the US
Army. (Also see Warrant Officers, below.)

Non-Com
See NCO, above.

Omaha
The code name for one of the beaches invaded on D-Day (the one
where Milo Flaten landed). The others were code-named Gold,
Juno, Utah and Sword.

Ordnance
Ammunition, explosives.

PA
Public Address system.

Packet
A US Army temporary group made up of troops from different units
traveling to the same general area.

Parapet
The loose soil around the rim of a foxhole.

Pillbox
A stone and metal blockhouse used by the German army in WWII
to conceal its soldiers but allow them to fire weapons through open
slits. They were above-ground, as opposed to bunkers, which were
usually partly buried.

Platoon
A US Army unit containing three squads.

PLT
See Platoon, above.

POW
Prisoner of War

PT
Physical Training

PTSD
Post-Traumatic Stress Disorder; the present name for adverse physical and psychological conditions arising after experiencing traumatic experiences; not uncommon among soldiers who have been in combat. Usually occurs sometime after the person is out of combat, whereas Battle Fatigue manifests while the person is in combat.

PX
Post Exchange; a general store run by the Army, located on an Army Base.

R and R
Rest and Recreation, or Rest and Recuperation; in the military, R and R refers to time away from fighting or other military duties.

Receiver
That part of a rifle or gun that receives, or holds, its ammunition.

Recon
Short for reconnaissance; getting information about enemy activities, often surreptitiously.

Regiment
A US Army unit containing three battalions.

Reich
German term for empire or realm.

Replacement Depot
An Army installation where soldiers are housed before being
shipped out to permanent assignments; GIs called them repple
depples (and sometimes repo depos).

Repple Depple
Slang name for Replacement Depot; see above.

RGT
See Regiment, above.

Salvo
See Barrage, above.

Sausage
In WWII, a large fenced-in holding pen for Allied soldiers about to
embark on the invasion of France.

Semaphore Flags
Small bicolored flags attached to two- to three-foot poles. A
signalman used them to send messages by holding them in various
positions to indicate numbers and letters of the alphabet.

SHAEF
Supreme Headquarters, American Expeditionary Force; General
Eisenhower's command of the Allied Forces fighting in Europe.

Shell shock
See Battle Fatigue, above.

Shrapnel
Hot, jagged pieces of metal projected outward from exploding
cannon shells, grenades, rockets and bombs.

Shuttle March
A method of moving soldiers involving trucking troops for a distance (perhaps five miles), marching them the same distance, and alternating those modes until the men reach their destination. Also called Motor March.

Siegfried Line
A 400-mile-long defensive line made up of pill boxes, tank traps and bunkers which Hitler built to prevent the Allies from advancing into Germany.

Skirmish Line
A line of skirmishers, soldiers involved in a particular battle or engagement.

Snafu
Situation normal, all (fouled) up, a phrase commonly used by GIs to describe mistakes and messes.

Squad
The smallest of permanently staffed infantry formations in WWII, usually consisting of ten men, a Squad Leader (a staff sergeant), and an Assistant Squad Leader (a sergeant).

SS
Schutzstaffel, or protective squadron; originally Hitler's bodyguard, its units fought alongside regular German Army troops in WWII. Some SS units committed atrocities and war crimes, including those in the Nazi death camps.

Sword
The code name of one of the D-Day beaches.

TDY
Temporary Duty, as with a unit not the soldier's primary assignment.

Tracer
Every third bullet in a belt of machine gun ammunition; it was covered with a chemical that burned red after it was fired, giving the gunner a clear indication of where his shots were landing.

USO
United Service Organization; an entity formed in February, 1941, to provide rest and recreational activities for servicemen and women to keep their morale up. Eventually the term was used casually to describe any group offering a canteen, a show for servicemen and women, free meals, etc.

Utah
The code name of one of the D-Day beaches.

V-1 and V-2
German Rockets; see Buzz Bomb, above.

WAC
Women's Army Corps, the branch of Army service for women. Created in 1941 as WAAC (Women's Auxiliary Army Corps), its members went on full active service in 1943 and the name was changed to WAC. The corps existed until 1978, when women were integrated into the regular army.

Warrant Officer
An Army member ranking above a Master Sergeant, and below the lowest commissioned officer, a second lieutenant. Warrant Officers generally had a specific skill; for instance, in early WWII some aircraft pilots were warrant officers; later, all pilots were commissioned.

WWII
A common abbreviation of "World War Two."

XO
Executive Officer, usually the second-in-command of a unit, responsible for its day-to-day operations.

Yankees or Yanks
British nickname for American soldiers.

Zig-zag Trench
A trench dug in a more or less z shape used by Germans in WWII for protection and as a base to shoot from.

Selected Bibliography

Ambrose, Stephen E. *Citizen Soldiers: The U.S. Army from the Normandy Beaches to The Bulge to the Surrender of Germany.* New York, NY: Simon & Schuster, 1997.

__________. *D-Day: June 6, 1944: The Climactic Battle of World War II.* New York, NY: Simon & Schuster, 1994.

Balkoski, Joseph. *Beyond The Beachhead: the 29th Infantry Division in Normandy.* Harrisburg, PA: Stackpole Books, 1989.

__________. *From Beachhead to Brittany: The 29th Infantry Division at Brest: August-September 1944.* Mechanicsburg, PA: Stackpole Books, 2013.

__________. *From Brittany to the Reich: The 29th Infantry Division in Germany: September-November 1944.* Mechanicsburg, PA: Stackpole Books, 2012.

__________. *Our Tortured Souls: The 29th Infantry Divi-

sion in the Rhineland: November-December 1944. Mechanicsburg, PA: Stackpole Books, 2008.

_______________. *The Last Roll Call: The 29th Infantry Division Victorious 1945*. Mechanicsburg, PA: Stackpole Books, 2015.

Blumenson, Martin. *Breakout and Pursuit*. Atlanta, GA: Whitman Publishing LLC, 2012.

Brinkley, Douglas, Director, and Haskew, Michael E., Editor. *The World War II Desk Reference*. Edison, NJ: Castle Books, 2008.

Ewing, Joseph H. *29 Let's Go: History of the 29th Infantry Division in World War II*. Washington, D.C.: Infantry Journal Press, 1948.

Hall, Anthony. *D-Day Day by Day: The Planning, the Landings, the Battles*. New York, NY: Chartwell Books, Inc., 2012.

Historical Division, War Department. *Omaha Beachhead (6 June-13 June 1944)*. Washington, D. C.: War Department, Historical Division, 1945.

Johns, Glover S., Jr. *The Clay Pigeons of St. Lo*. Mechanicsburg, PA: Stackpole Books, 2002.

Lande, D. A. *I Was with Patton: First-Person Accounts of WWII in George S. Patton's Command*. St. Paul, MN: Quarto Publishing Group, USA, 2002.

MacDonald, Charles B. *The Siegfried Line Campaign*. Washington, D.C., Center of Military History, United States Army, 1993.

Man, John. *The D-Day Atlas: The Definitive Account of the Allied Invasion of Normandy*. New York, NY: Facts on File, Inc., 1994.

Reynolds, Michael. *Eagles and Bulldogs in Normandy 1944: The American 29th Infantry Division from Omaha Beach to St. Lo, and the British 3rd Infantry Division from Sword Beach to Caen.* Havertown, PA: Casemate, 2003.

Index

Entries shown in bold indicate charts,
photos or maps